WARWICKSHIRE IN PHOTOGRAPHS

DAVE JENNINGS

AMBERLEY

First published 2018

Amberley Publishing
The Hill, Stroud
Gloucestershire, GL5 4EP

www.amberley-books.com

Copyright © Dave Jennings, 2018

The right of Dave Jennings to be identified as the Author of this work has been
asserted in accordance with the Copyrights, Designs and Patents Act 1988.

ISBN 978 1 4456 8395 9 (print)
ISBN 978 1 4456 8396 6 (ebook)

The images on page 11, 33, 37, 87 and 94 have been used by kind
permission of Warwickshire Country Parks. The image on page 95 has been
used by kind permission of Collegiate Church of St Mary, Warwick. And the
image on page 41 has been used by kind permission of Draycote Water.

British Library Cataloguing in Publication Data.
A catalogue record for this book is available from the British Library.

Origination by Amberley Publishing.
Printed in the UK.

ACKNOWLEDGEMENTS

I would like to thank my girlfriend, Sharon, for her help and support. She walked many a countryside mile with me and was always there to give me the prompt I sometimes needed to sort through the photos. Without you this book would never have happened.

Also thank you to members of the 'Coventry and Warwickshire Photography' Facebook group for helping with places to visit, and to Glyn Diablo Parry for the guided walk around Ilmington.

I would also like to thank Amberley Publishing for approaching me and giving me this opportunity.

ABOUT THE PHOTOGRAPHER

My love for photography was ignited after Sharon bought me a camera one Christmas. After that an hour-long walk would start taking two hours. Flowers were only bought if I was photographing them, air shows and motor sport events were viewed through the lens, and I started to see the world in apertures, ISOs and shutter speeds.

I have had photographs published in local papers, the BBC website, magazines and in motor sport promotional material.

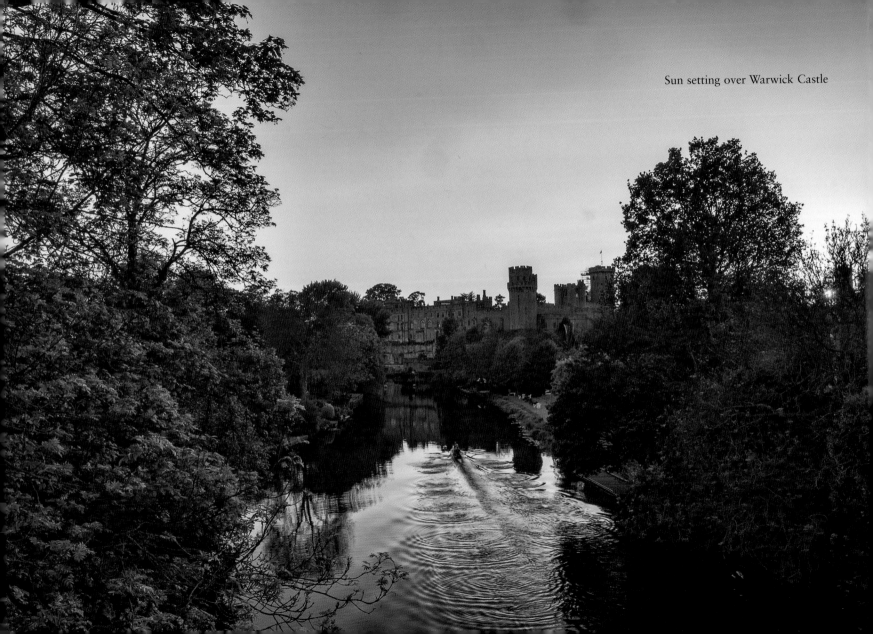

Sun setting over Warwick Castle

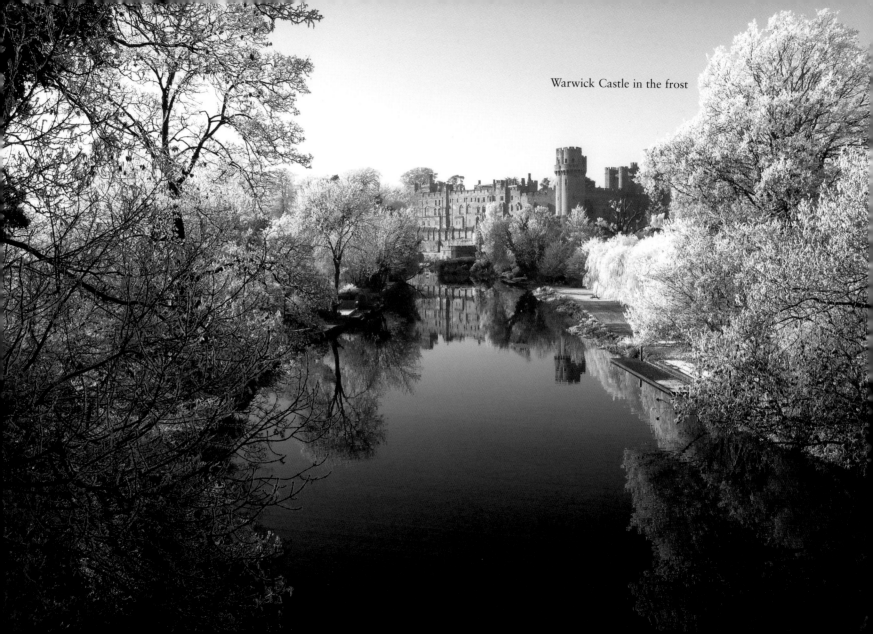

Warwick Castle in the frost

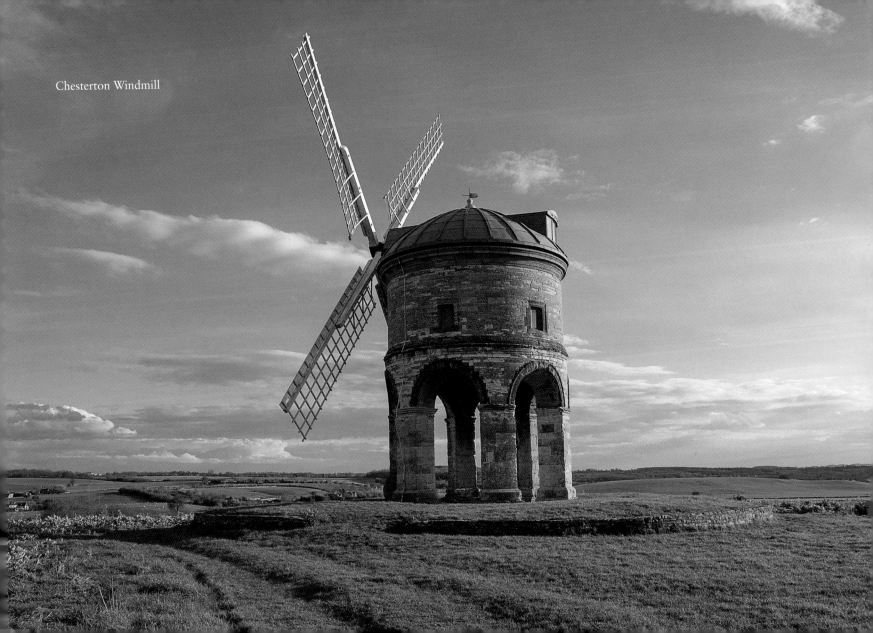

Chesterton Windmill

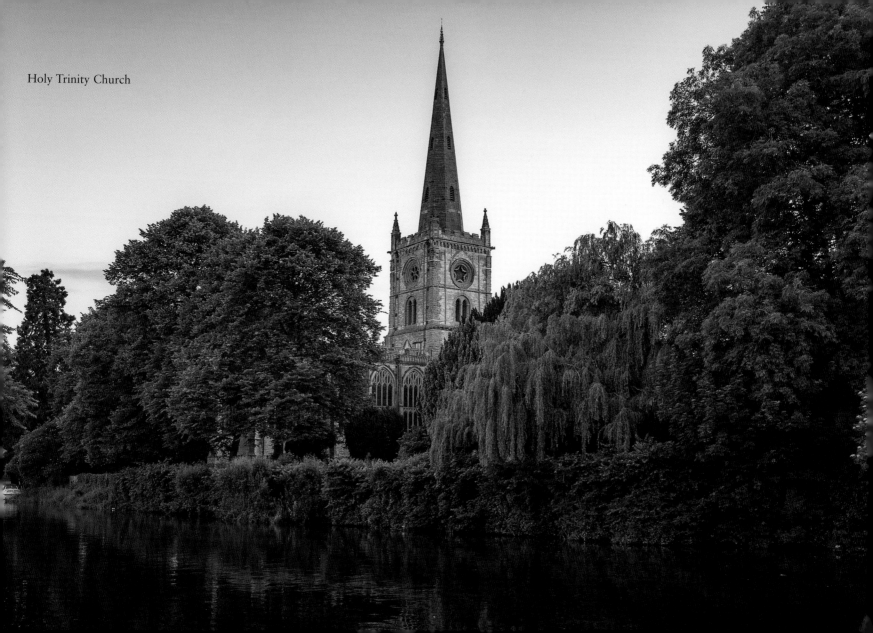
Holy Trinity Church

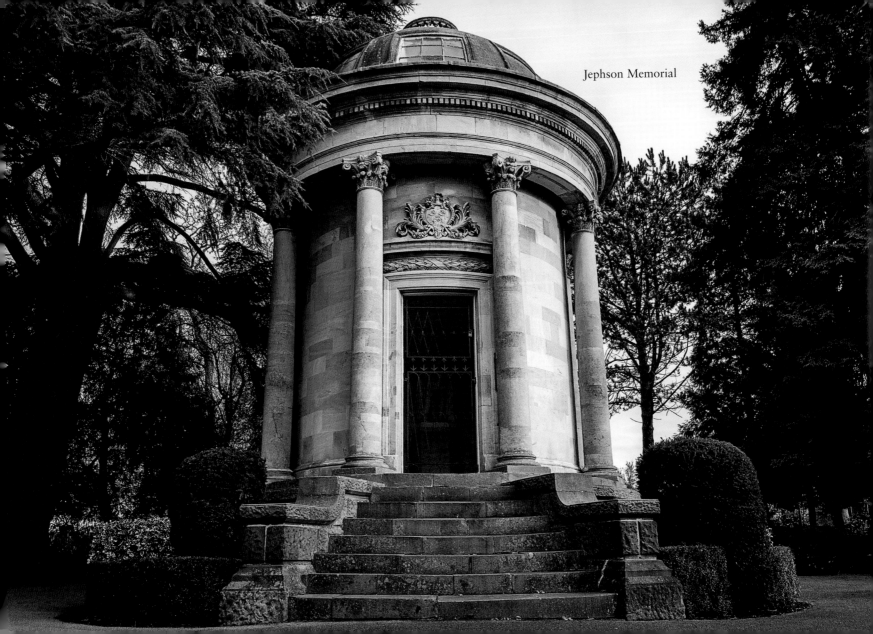

Jephson Memorial

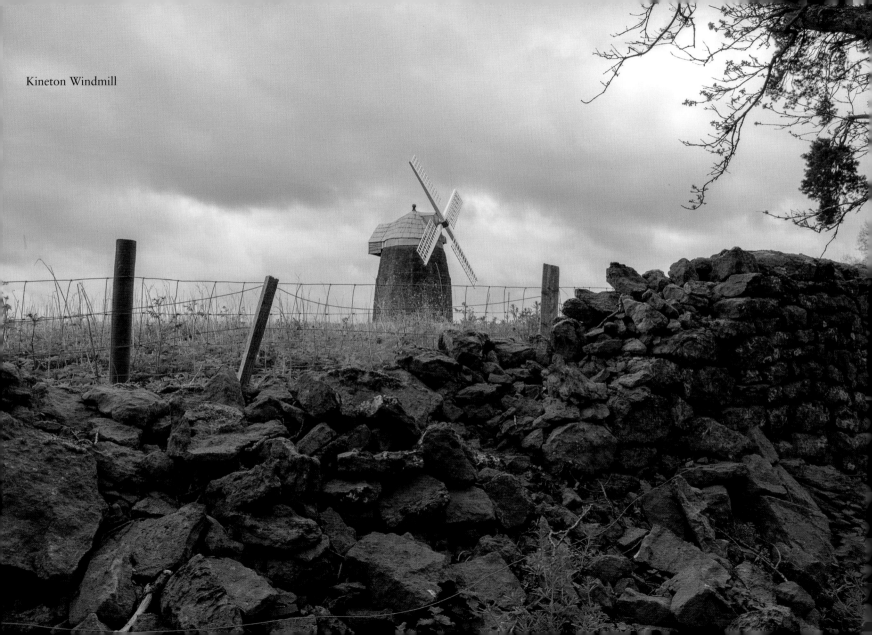

Kineton Windmill

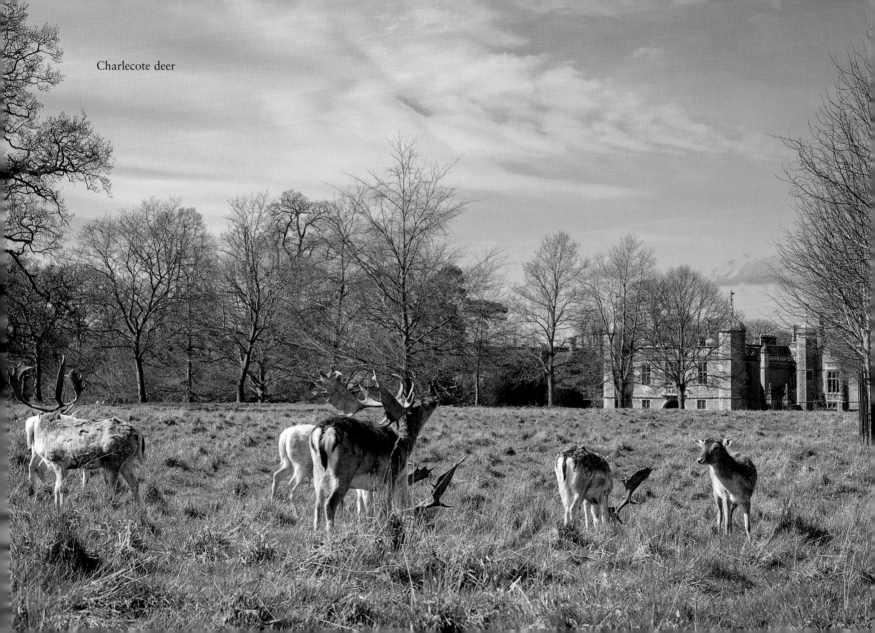

Charlecote deer

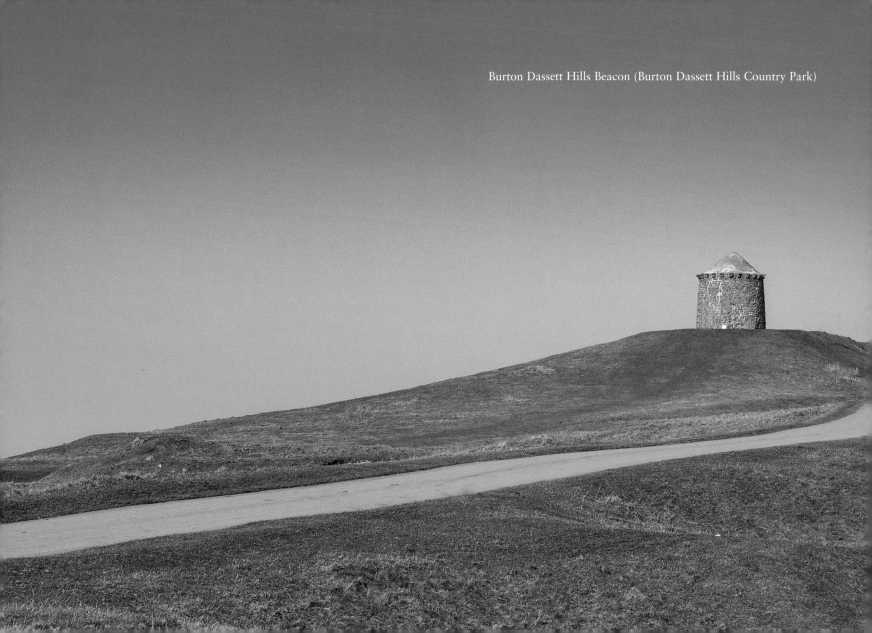

Burton Dassett Hills Beacon (Burton Dassett Hills Country Park)

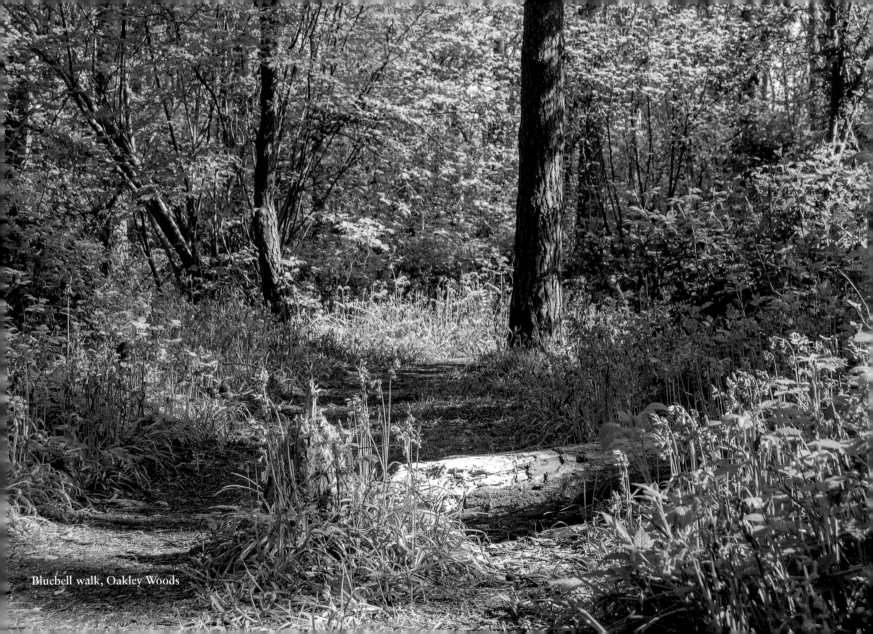

Bluebell walk, Oakley Woods

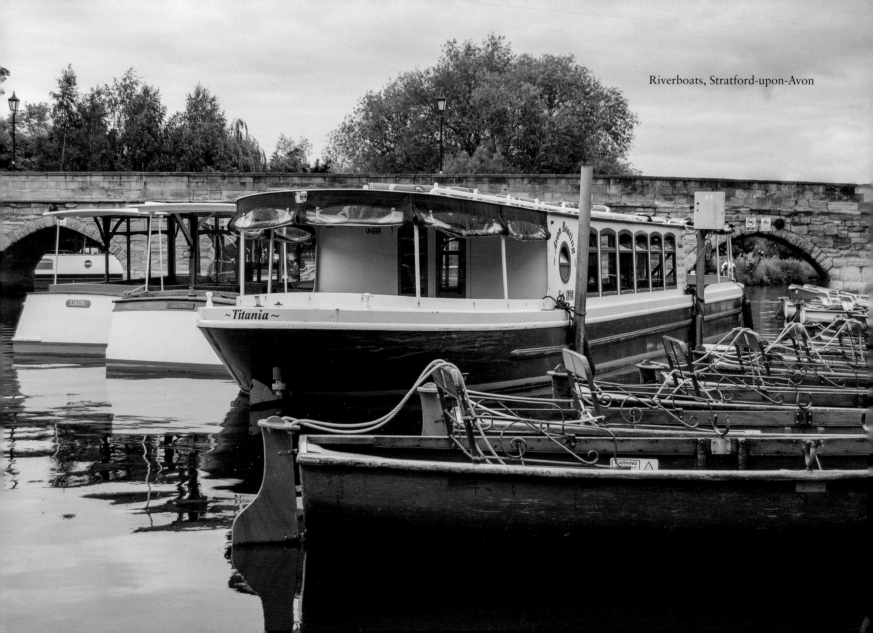

Riverboats, Stratford-upon-Avon

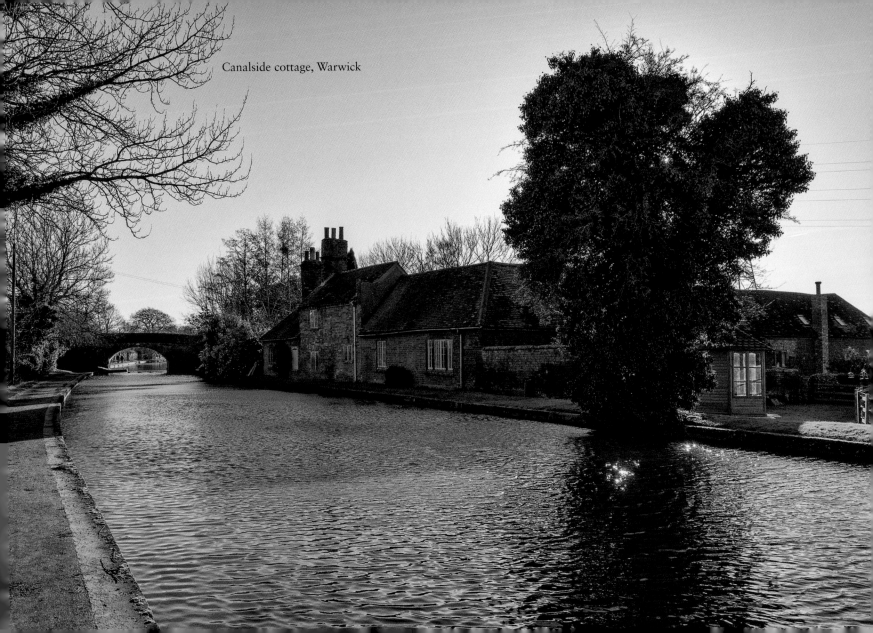

Canalside cottage, Warwick

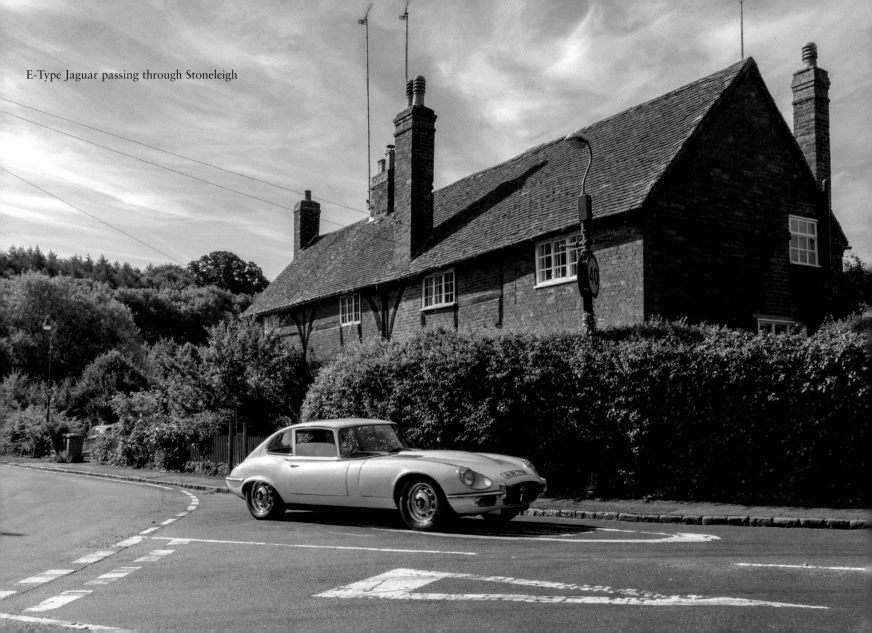

E-Type Jaguar passing through Stoneleigh

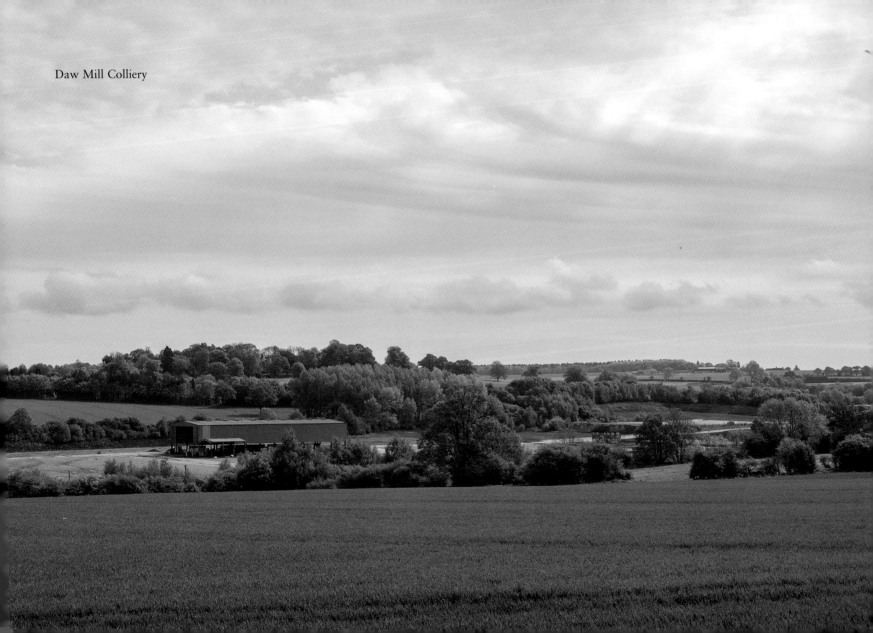

Daw Mill Colliery

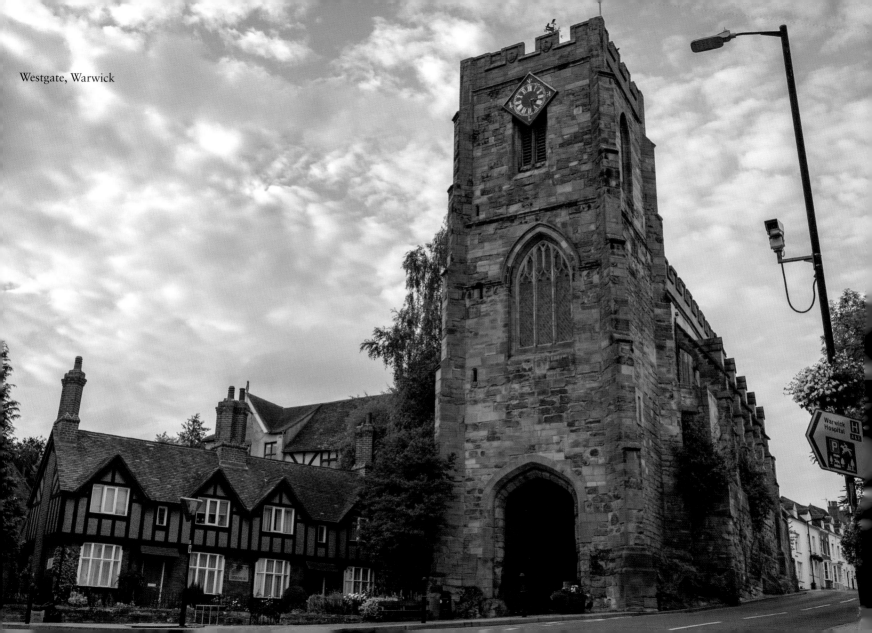

Westgate, Warwick

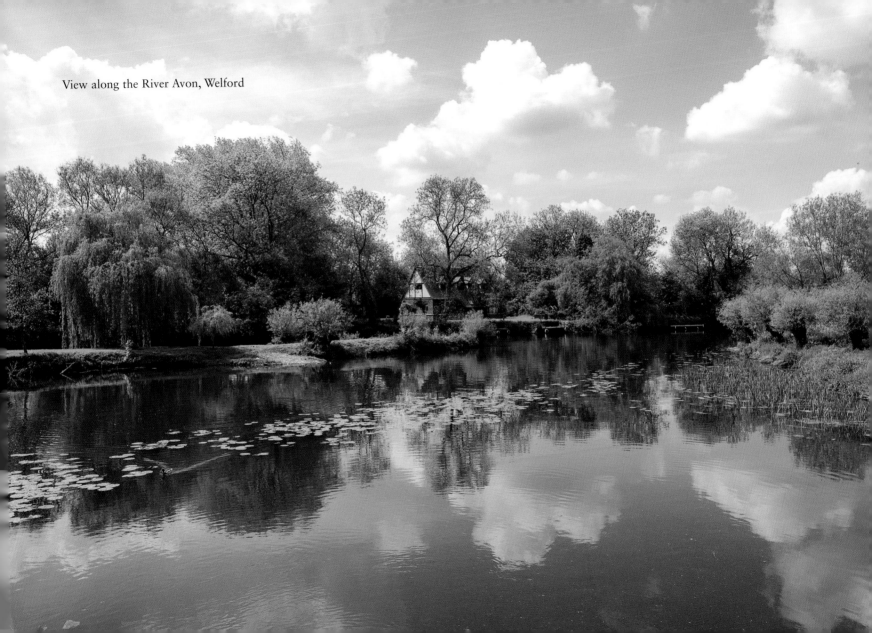

View along the River Avon, Welford

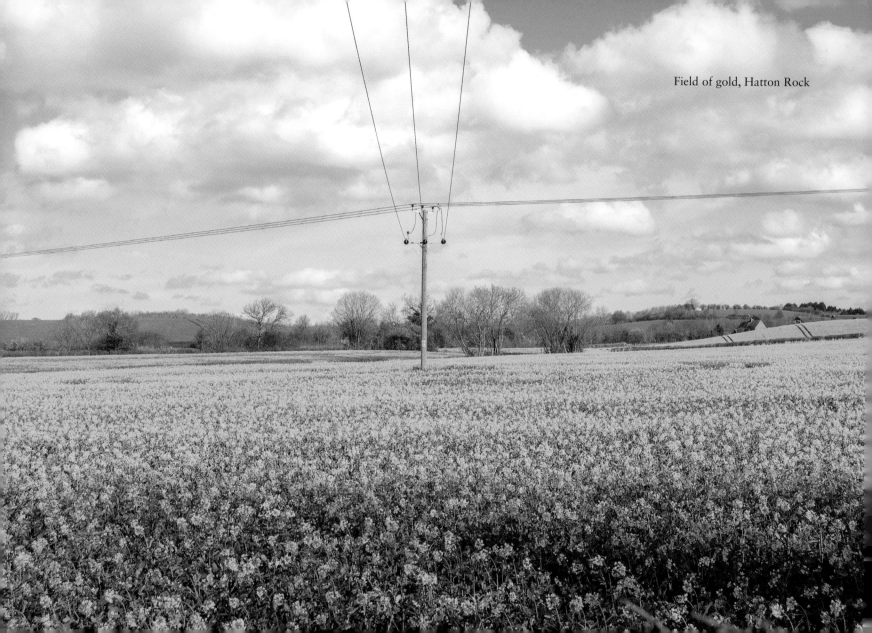

Field of gold, Hatton Rock

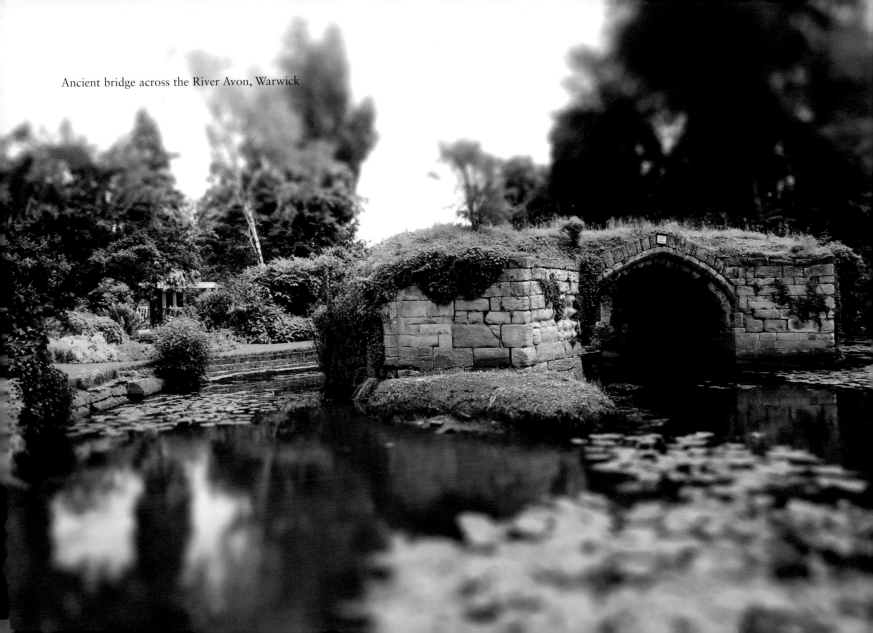

Ancient bridge across the River Avon, Warwick

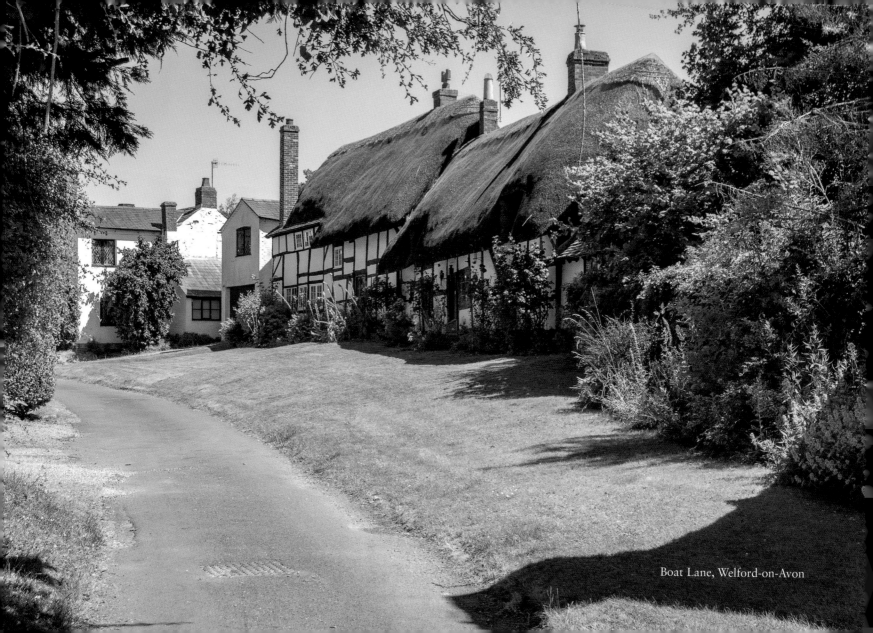

Boat Lane, Welford-on-Avon

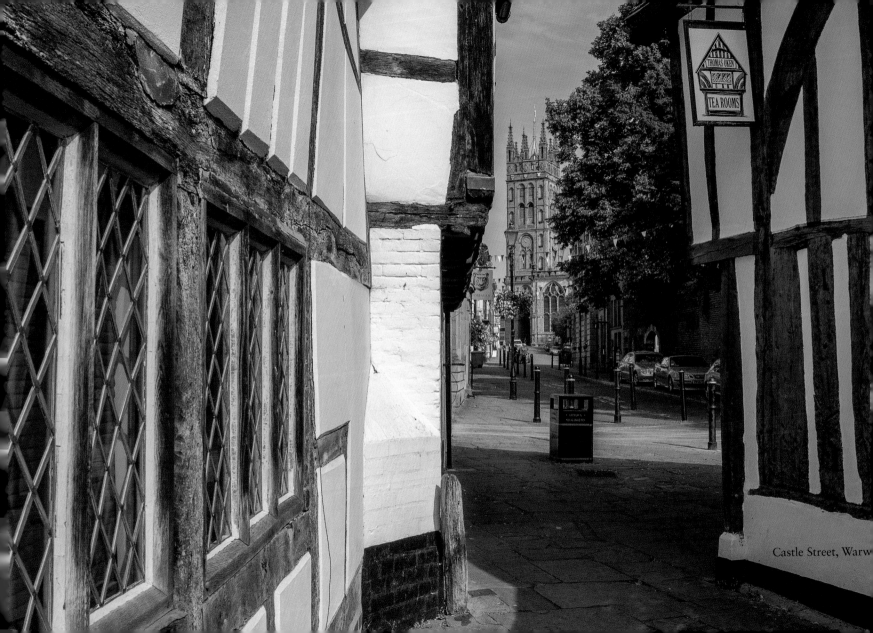

THOMAS OKEN
TEA ROOMS

Castle Street, Warw

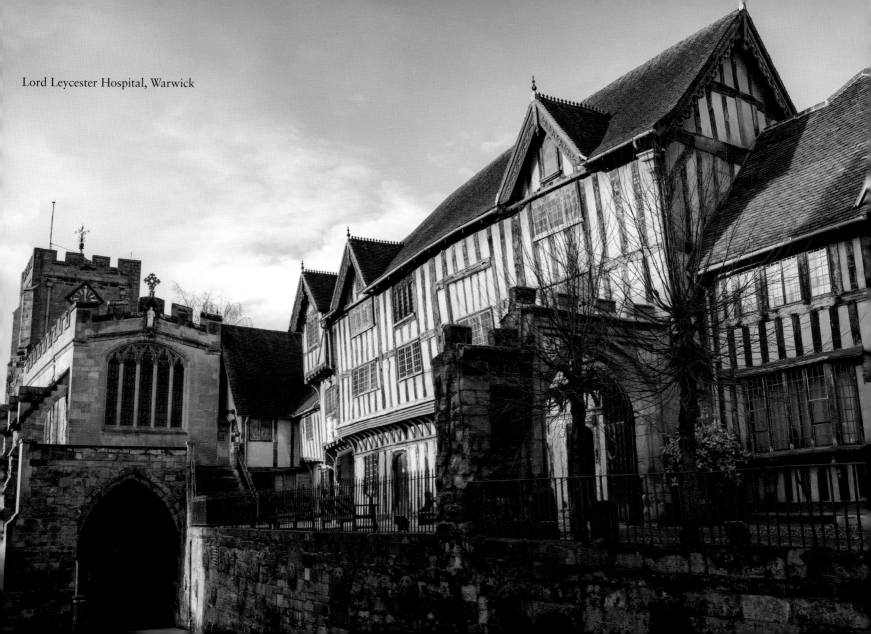

Lord Leycester Hospital, Warwick

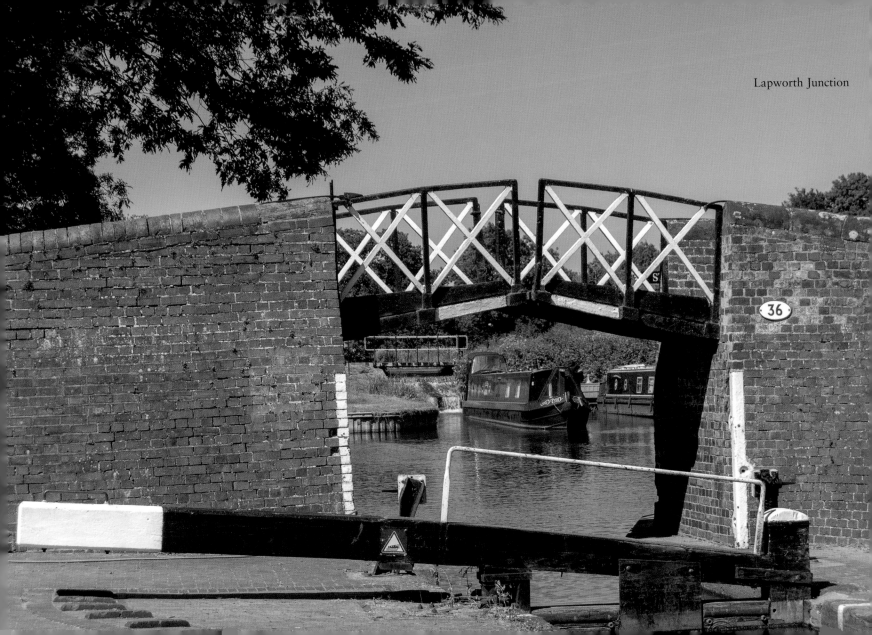

Lapworth Junction

36

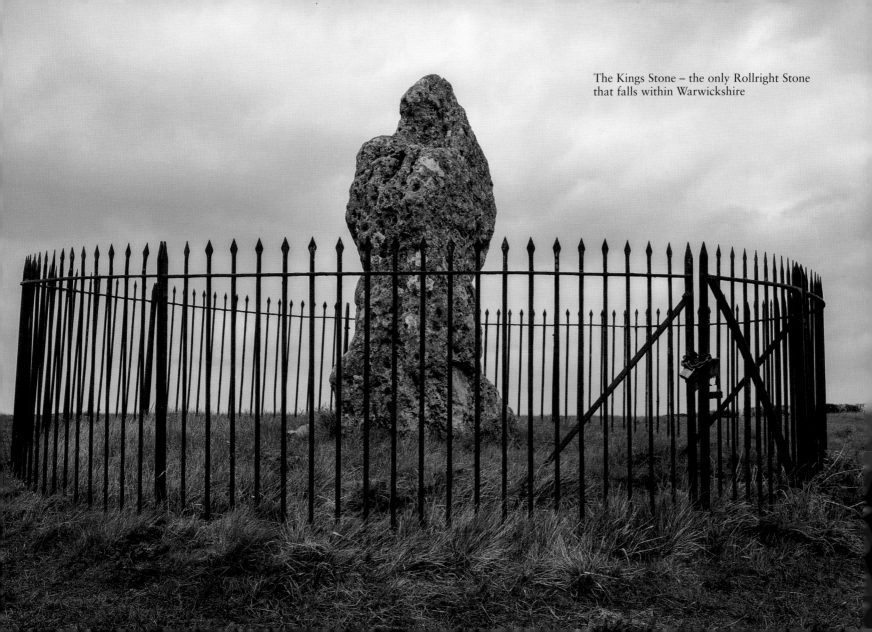

The Kings Stone – the only Rollright Stone
that falls within Warwickshire

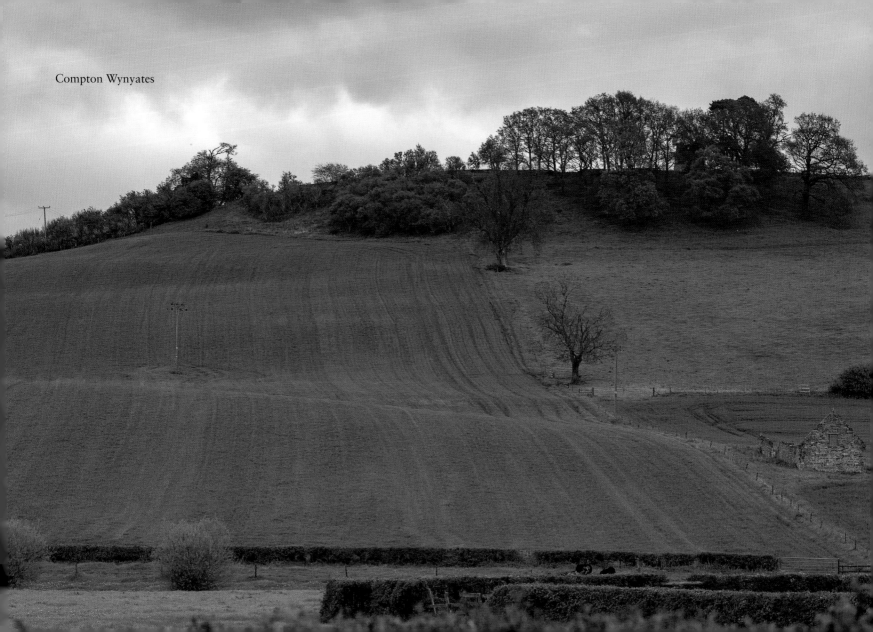

Compton Wynyates

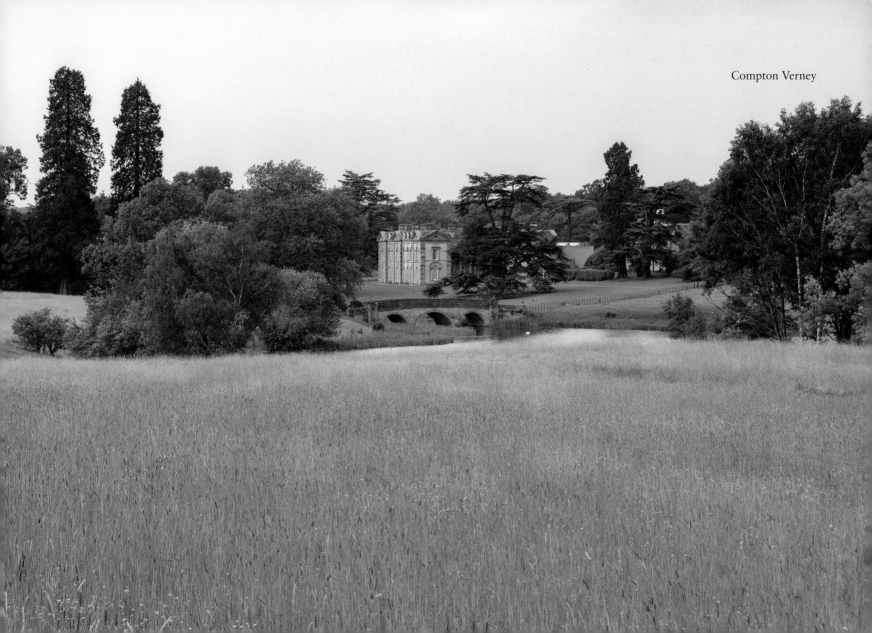

Compton Verney

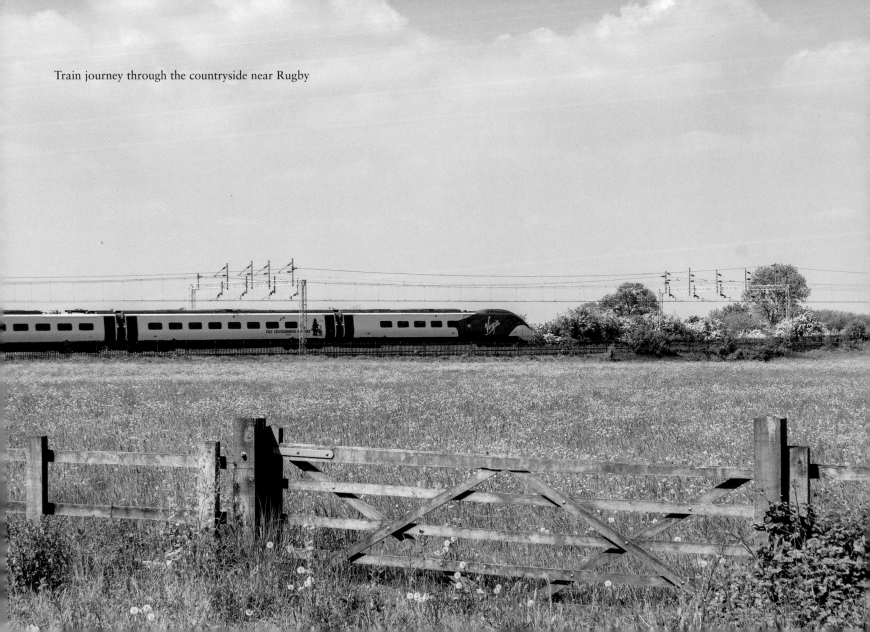

Train journey through the countryside near Rugby

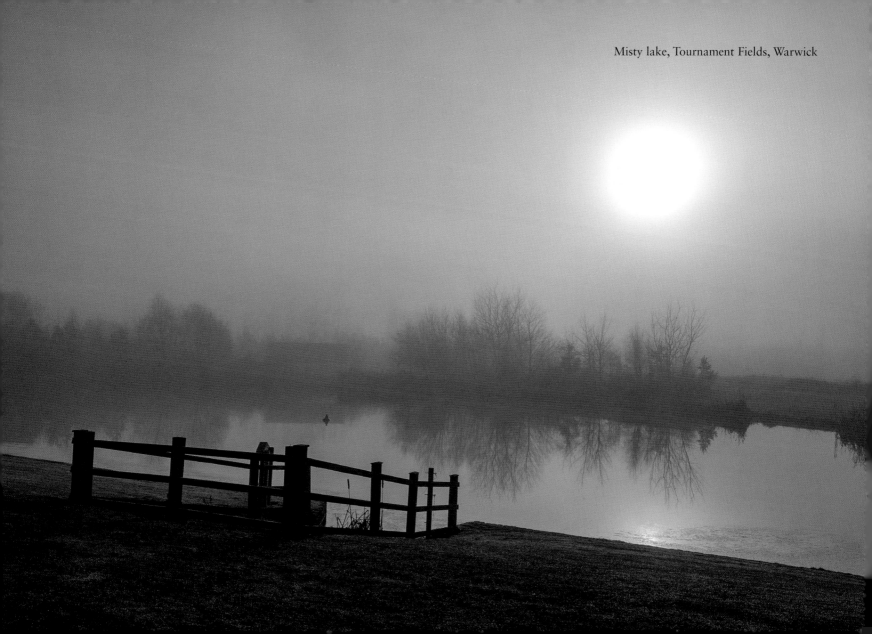
Misty lake, Tournament Fields, Warwick

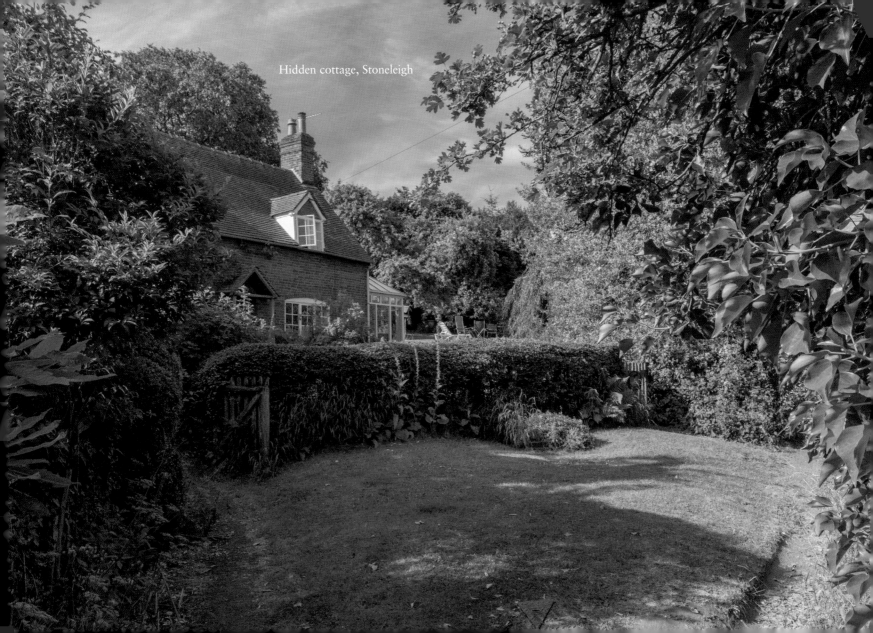

Hidden cottage, Stoneleigh

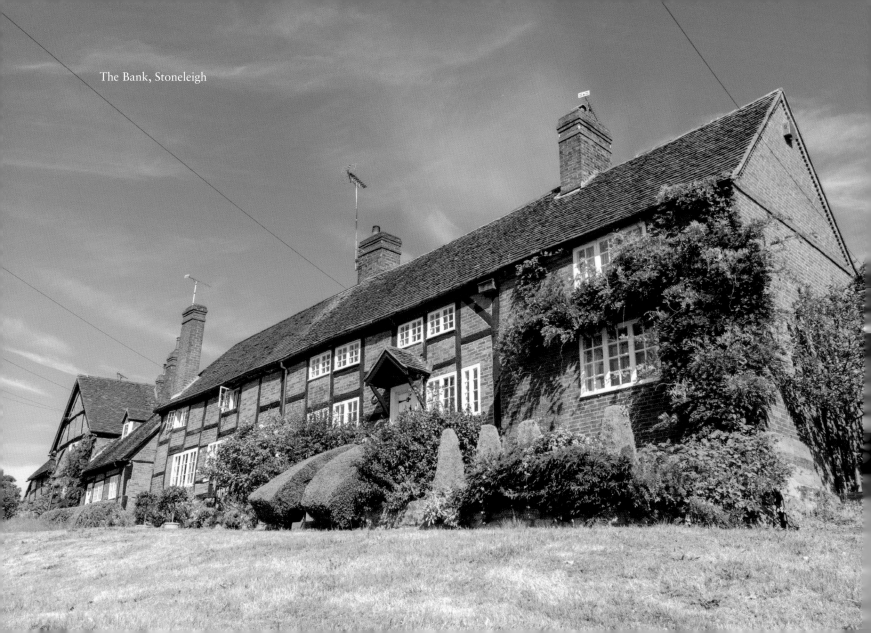

The Bank, Stoneleigh

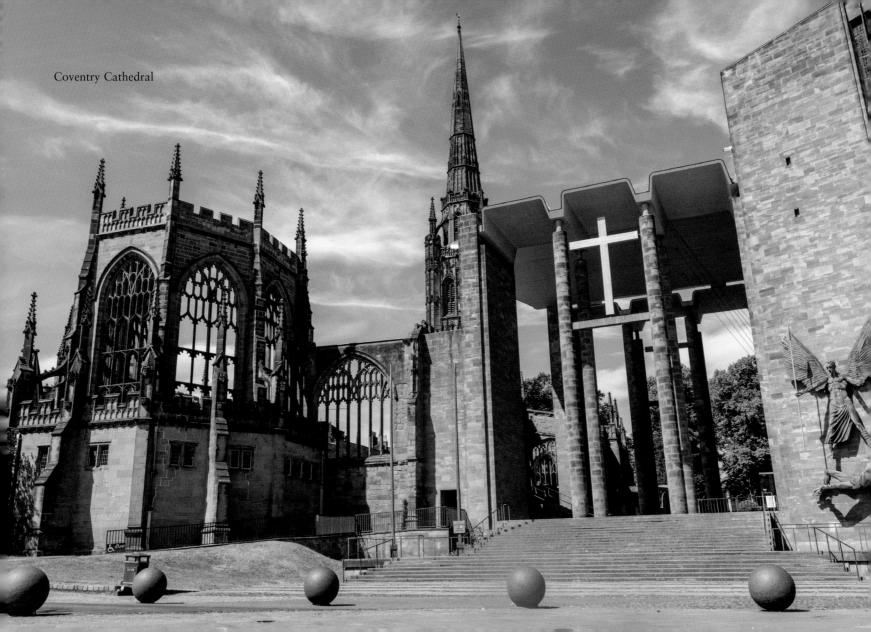

Coventry Cathedral

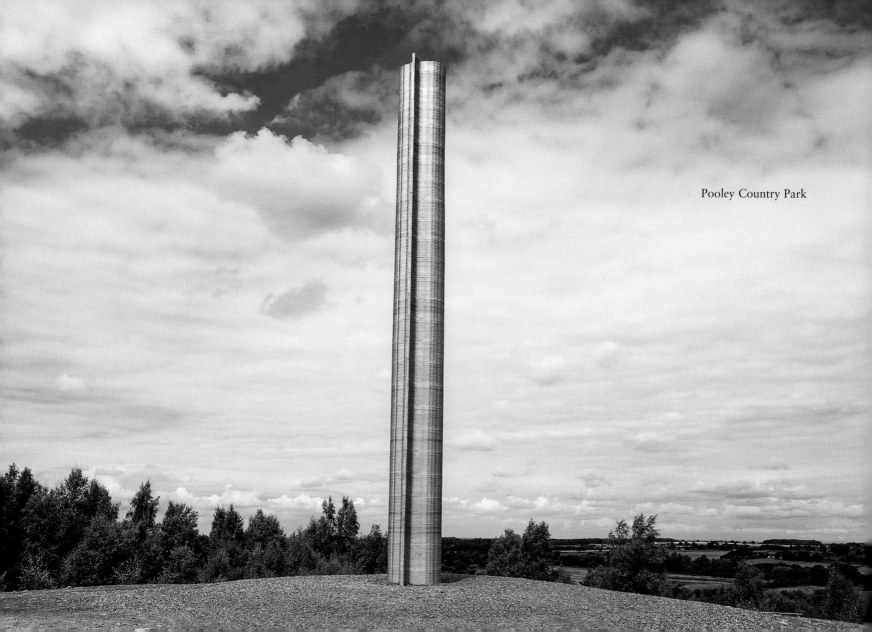

Pooley Country Park

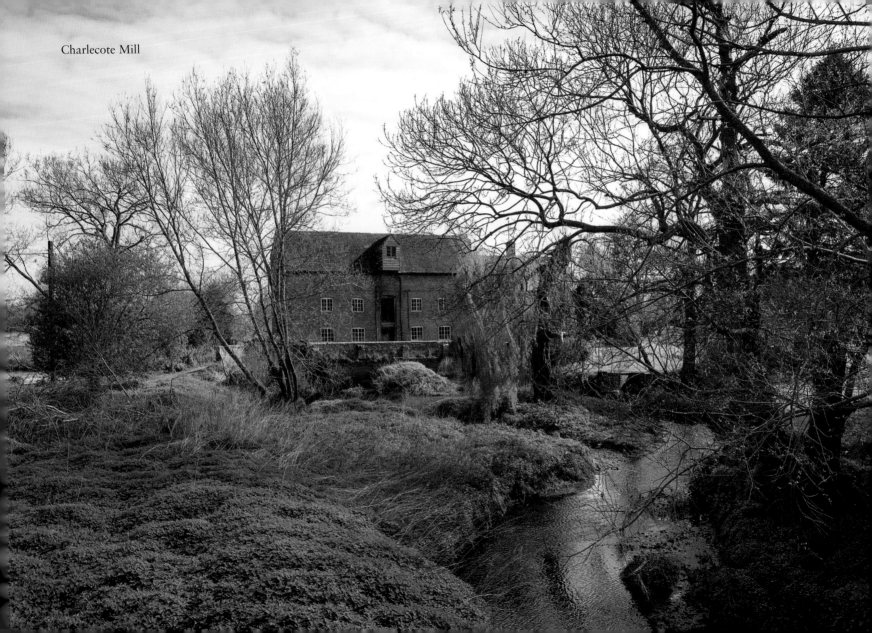
Charlecote Mill

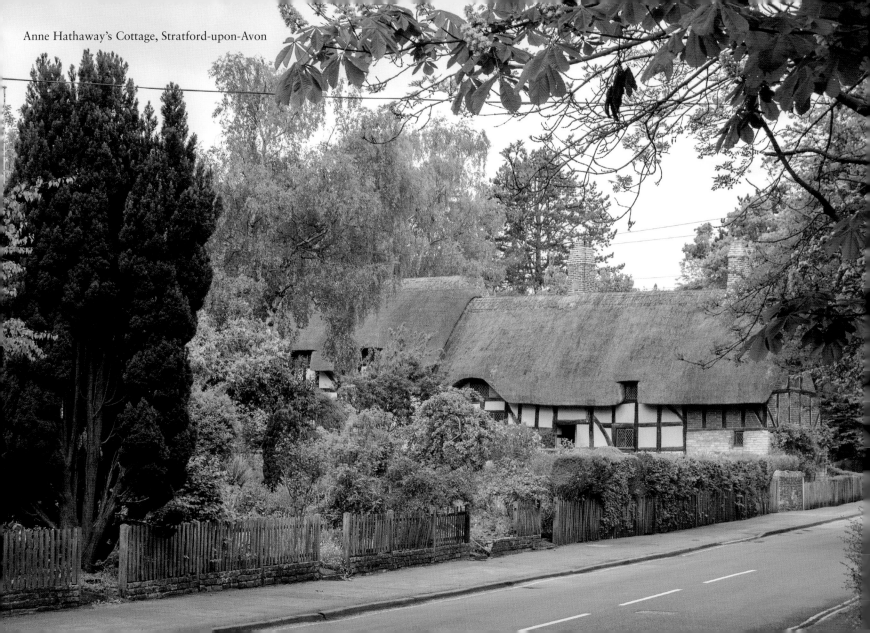

Anne Hathaway's Cottage, Stratford-upon-Avon

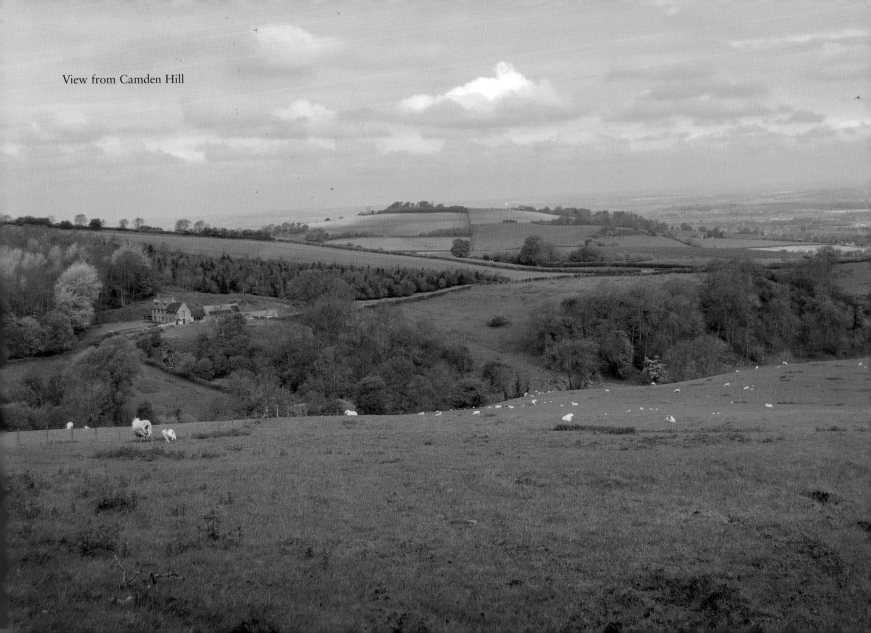

View from Camden Hill

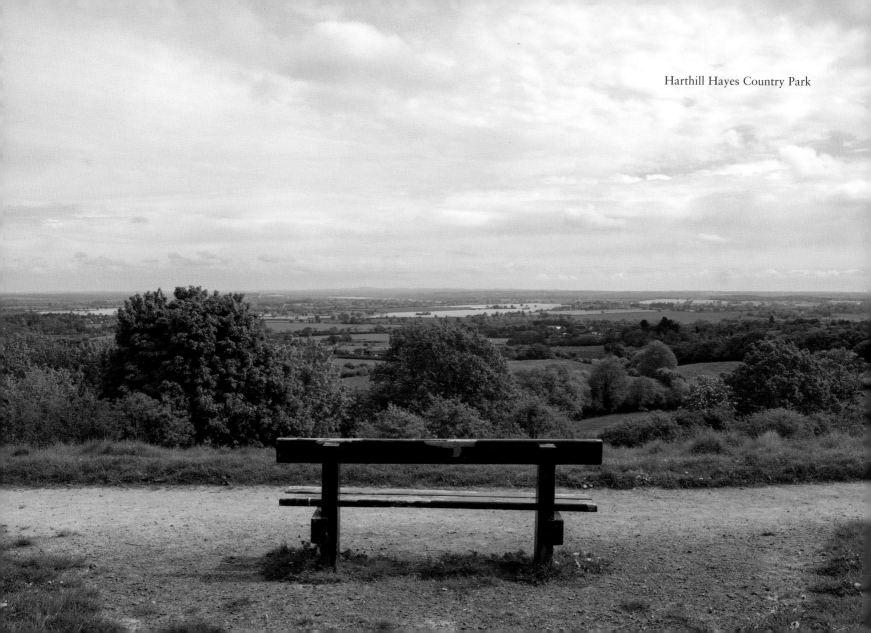

Harthill Hayes Country Park

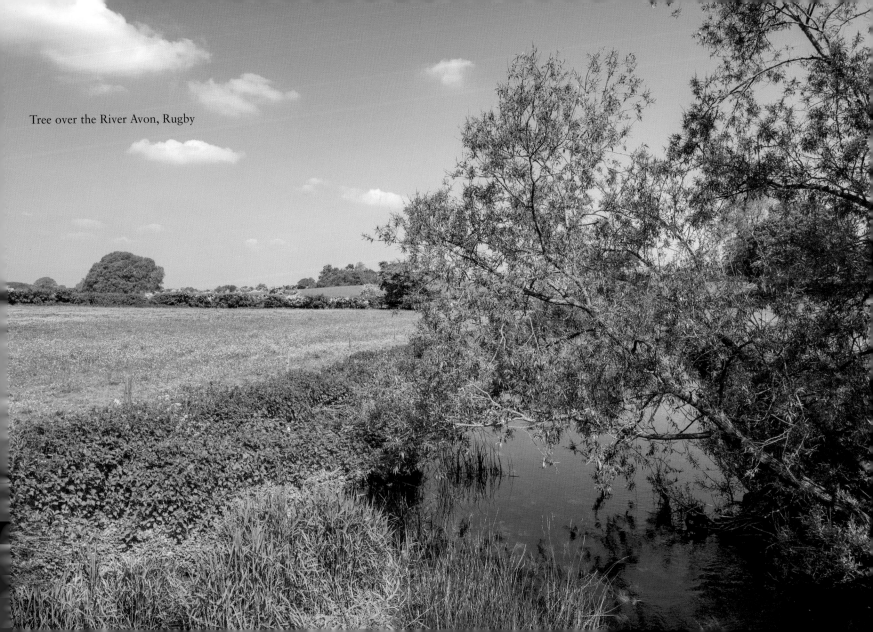

Tree over the River Avon, Rugby

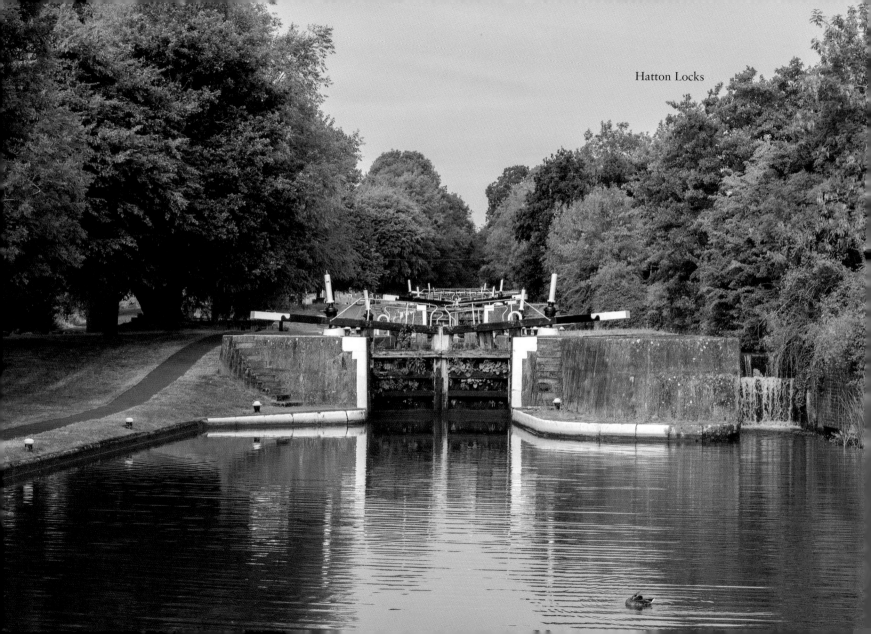

Hatton Locks

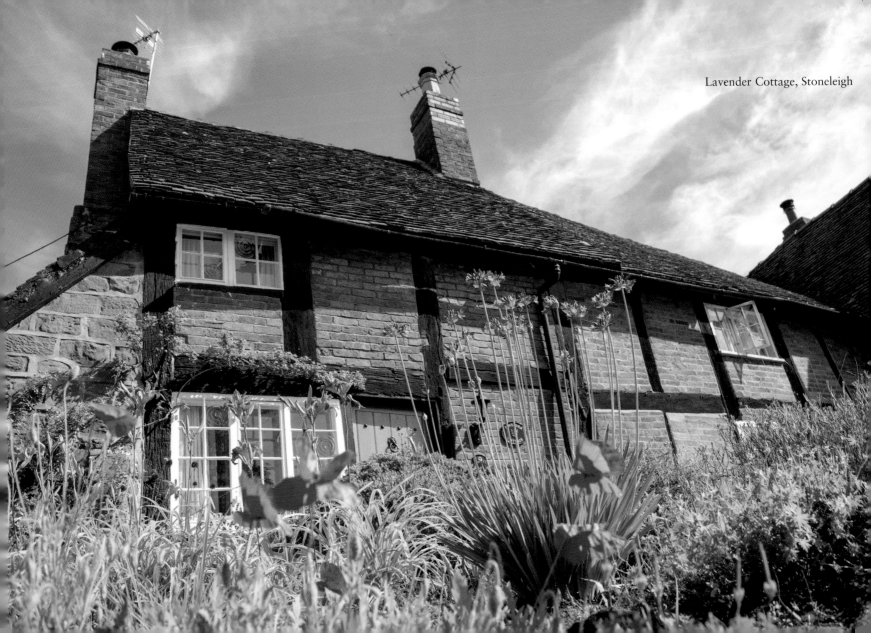

Lavender Cottage, Stoneleigh

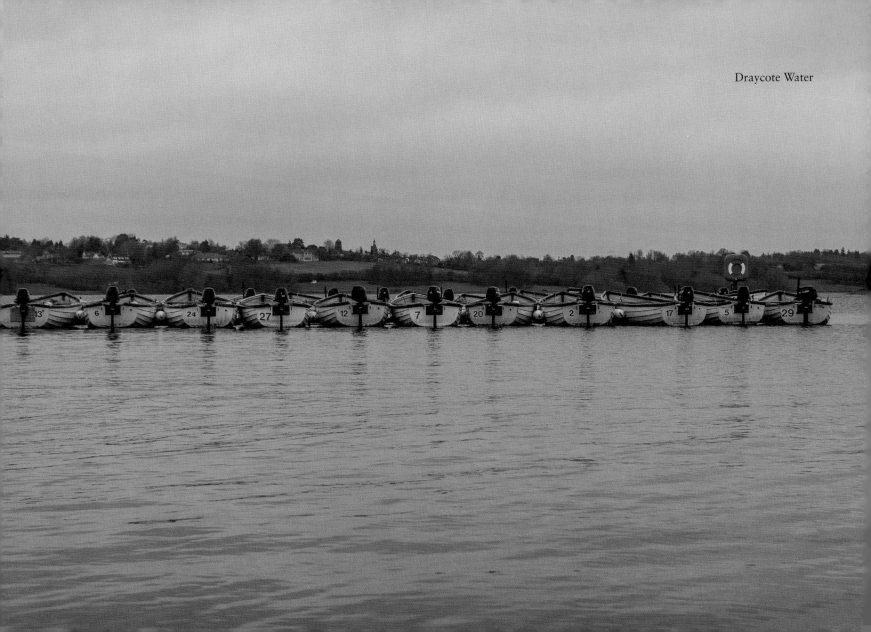

Draycote Water

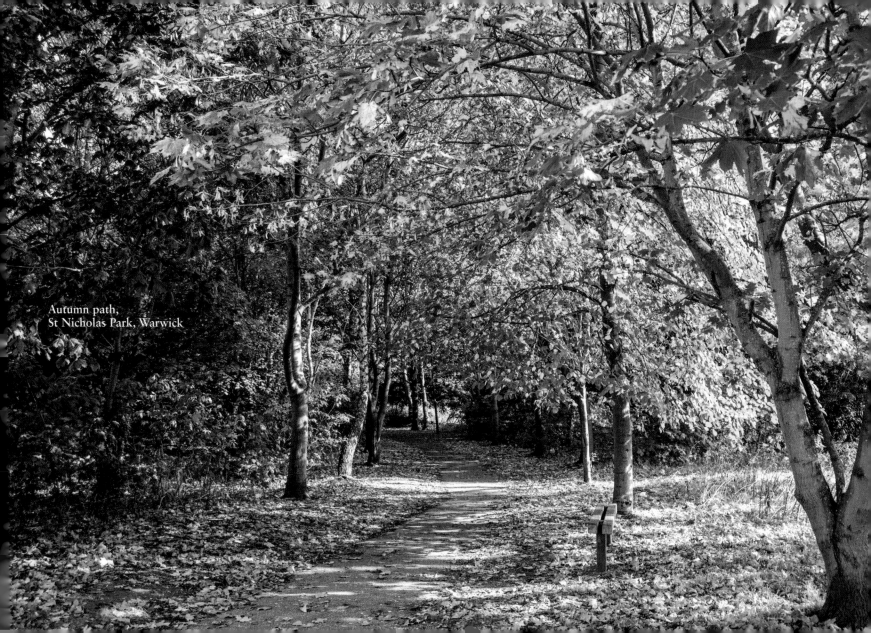

Autumn path,
St Nicholas Park, Warwick

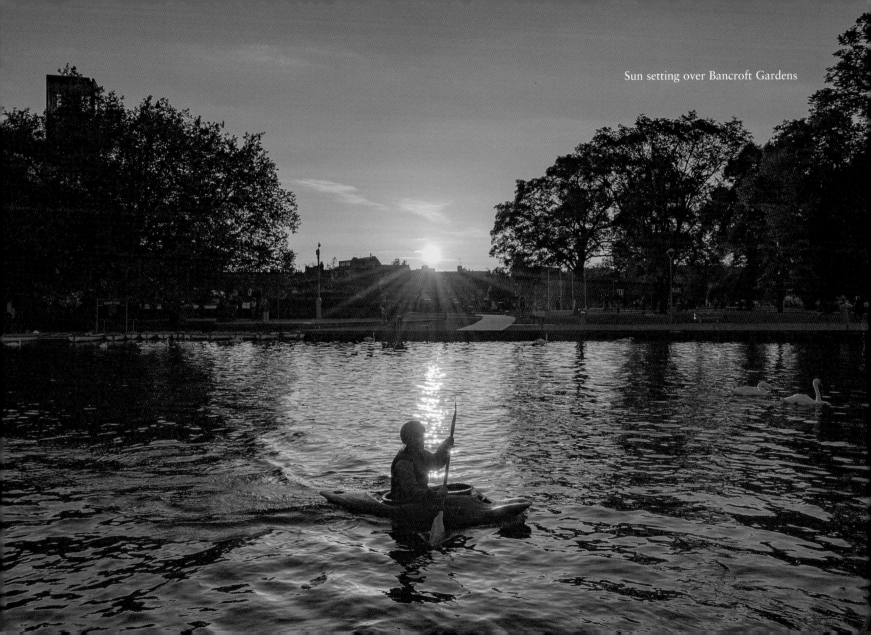

Sun setting over Bancroft Gardens

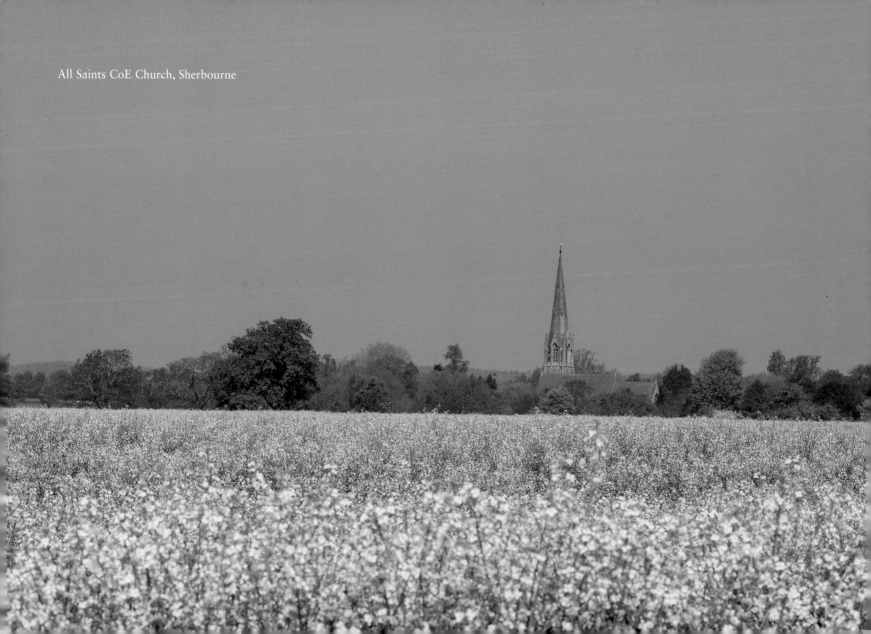

All Saints CoE Church, Sherbourne

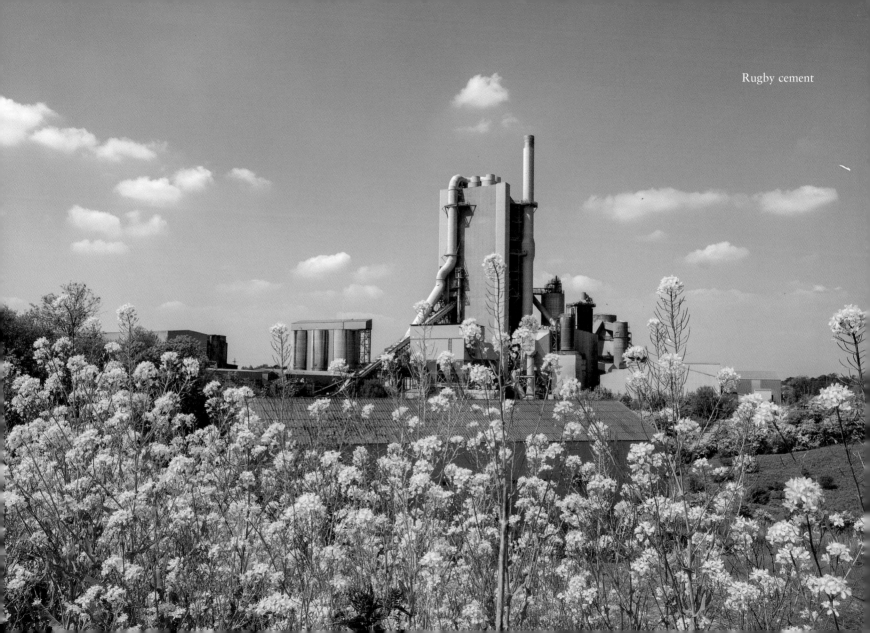

Rugby cement

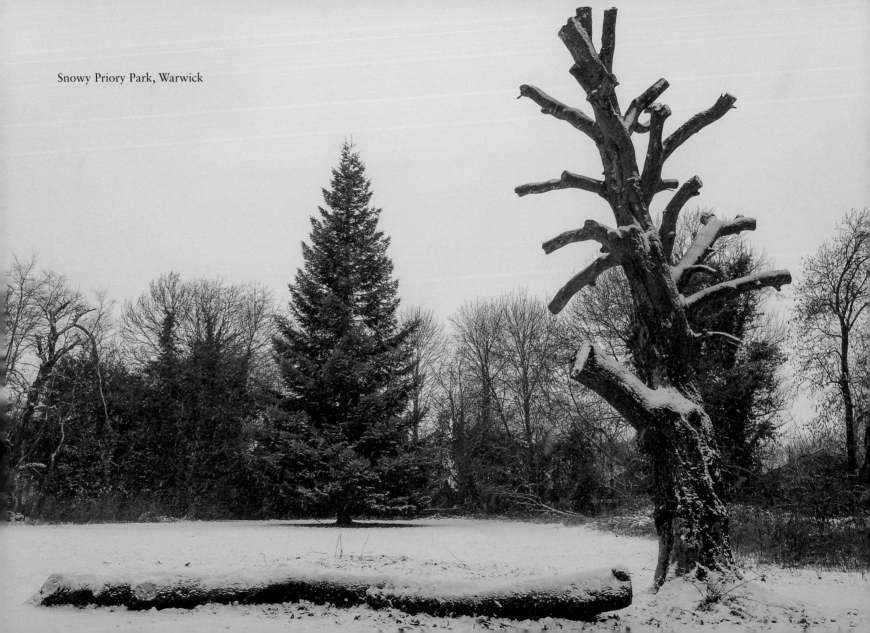

Snowy Priory Park, Warwick

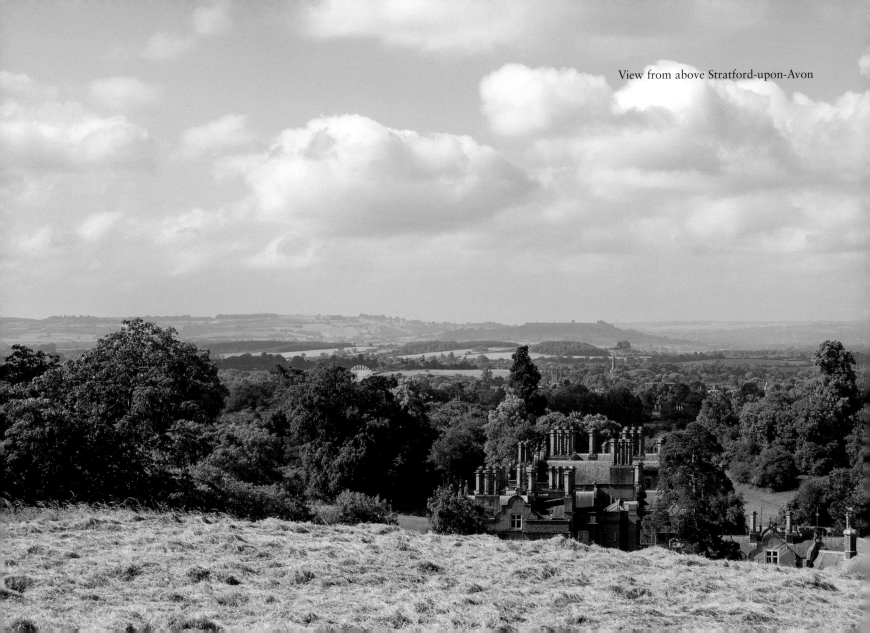
View from above Stratford-upon-Avon

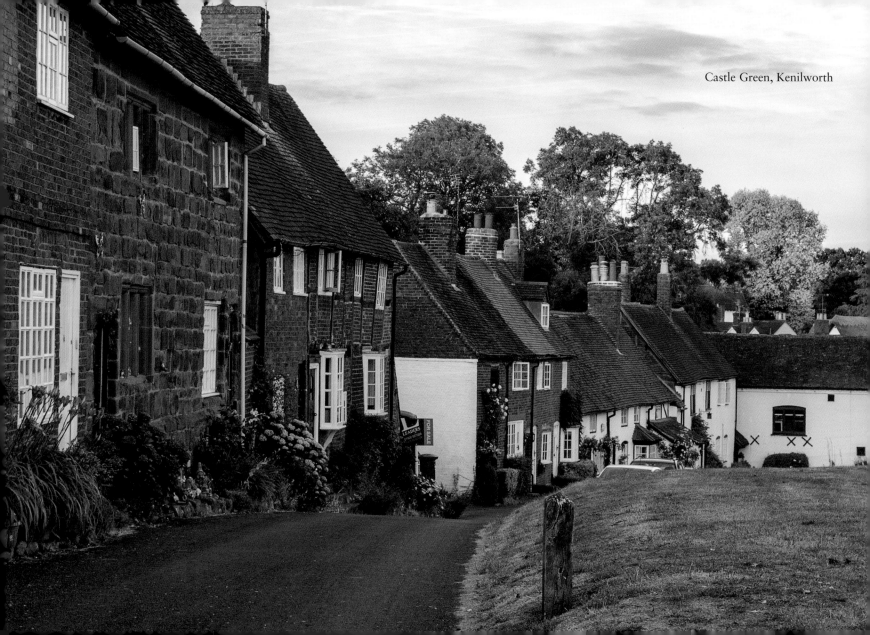

Castle Green, Kenilworth

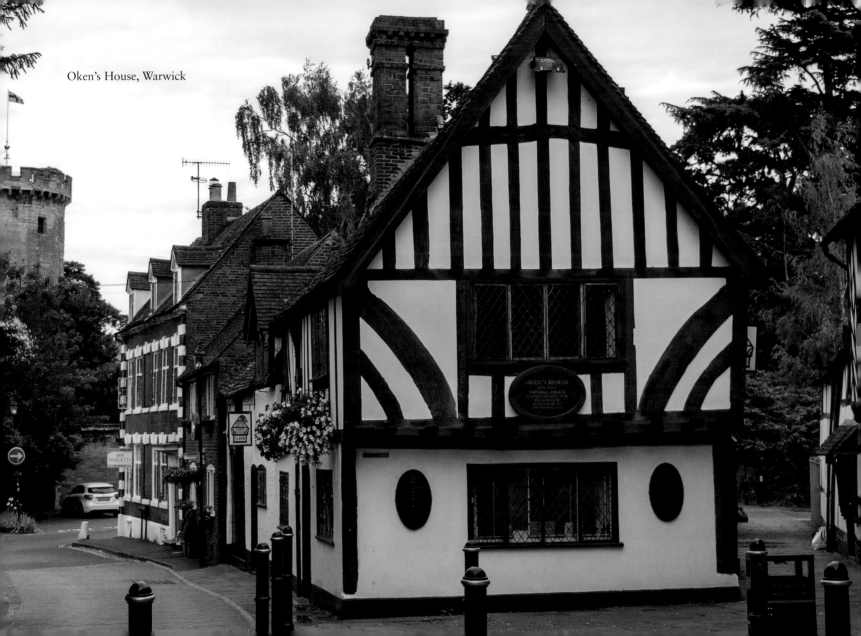

Oken's House, Warwick

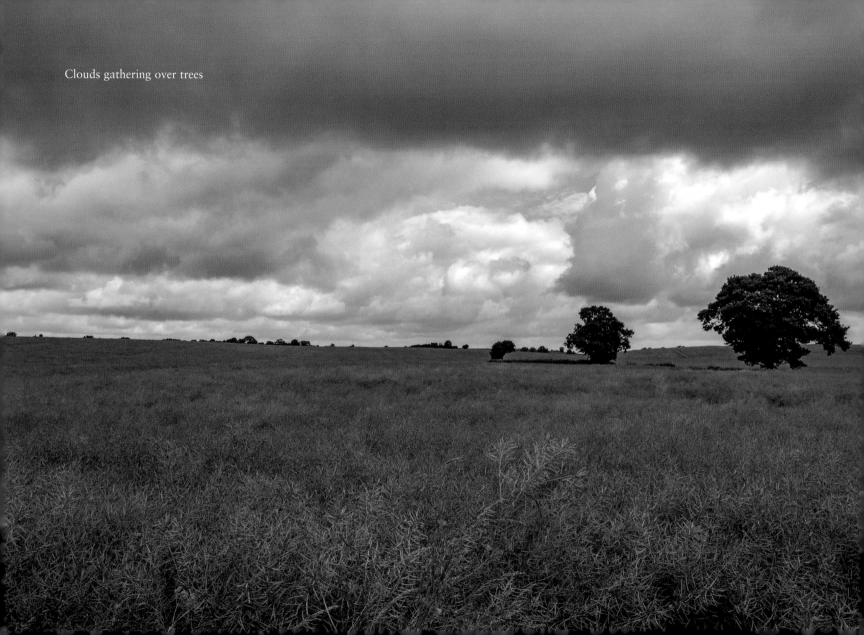

Clouds gathering over trees

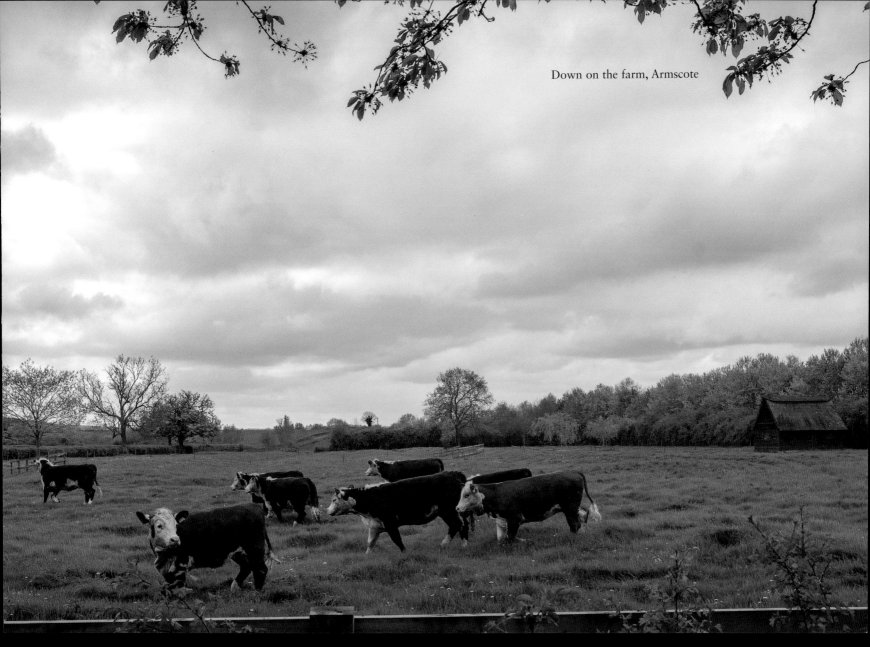

Down on the farm, Armscote

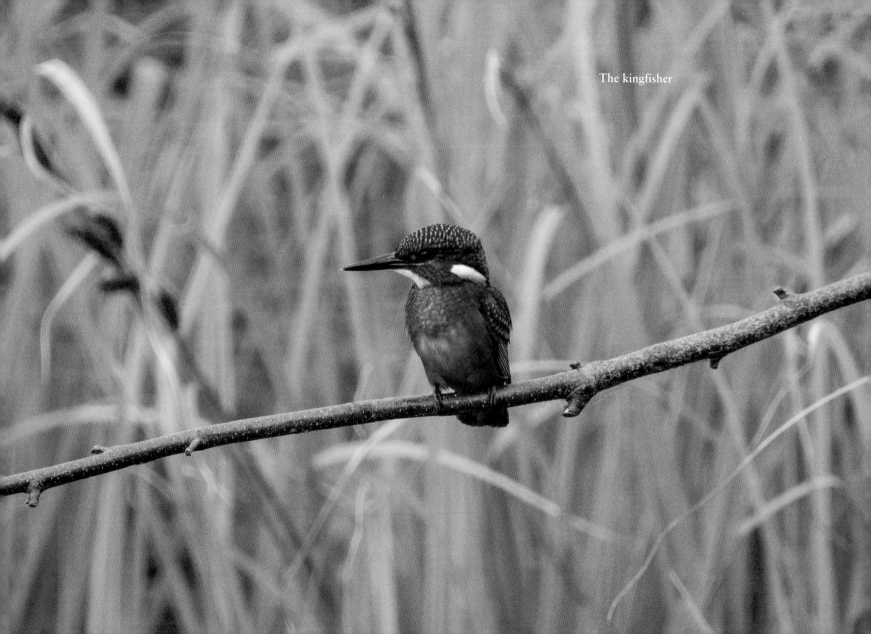

The kingfisher

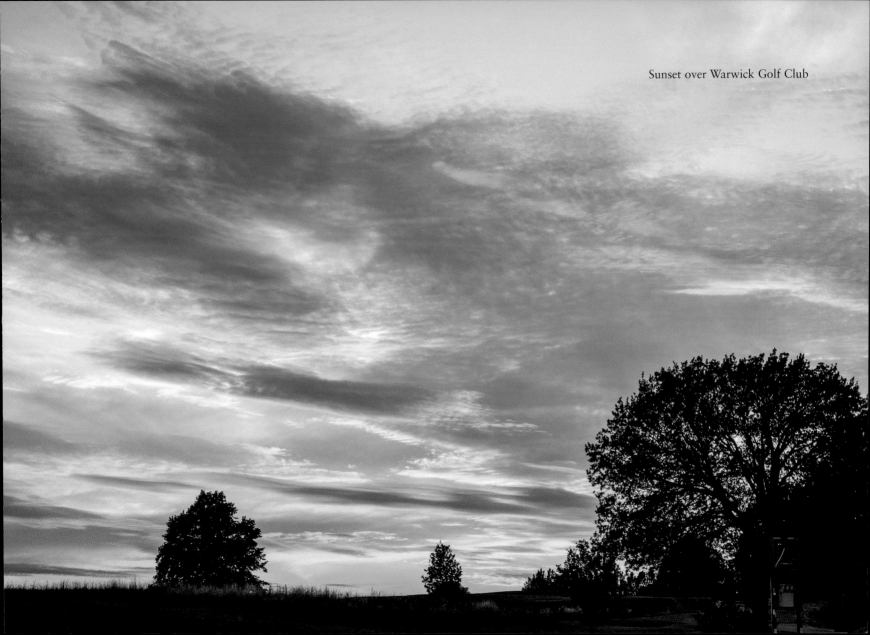

Sunset over Warwick Golf Club

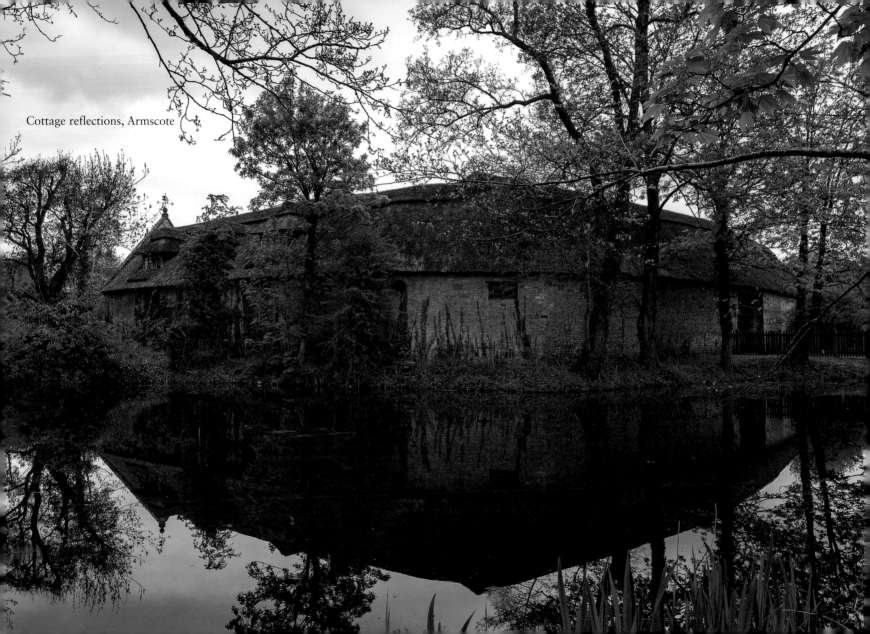

Cottage reflections, Armscote

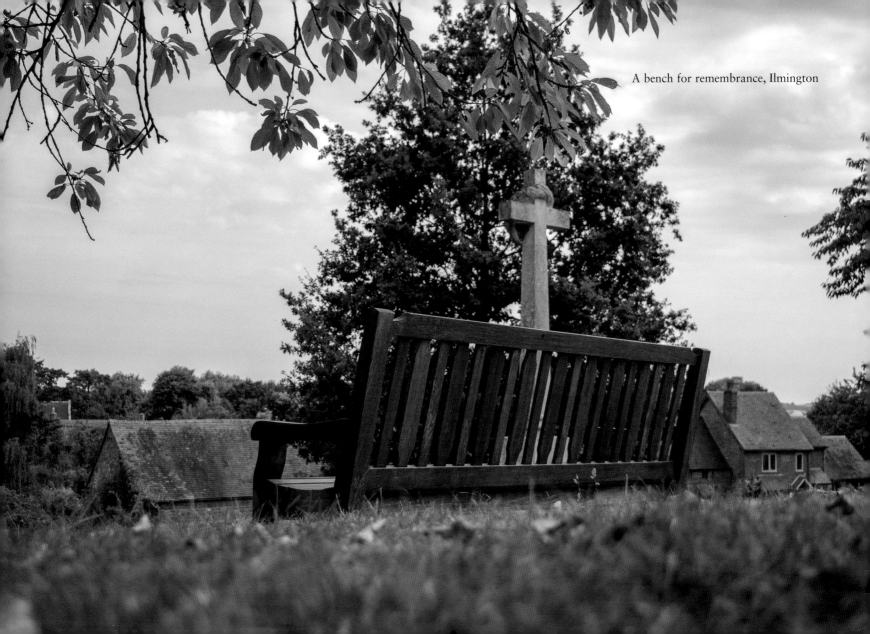

A bench for remembrance, Ilmington

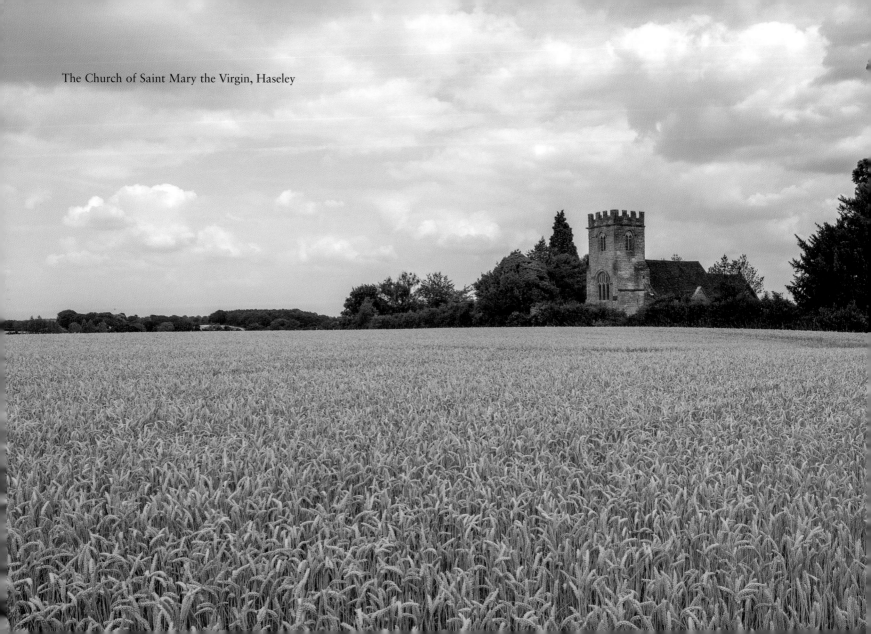

The Church of Saint Mary the Virgin, Haseley

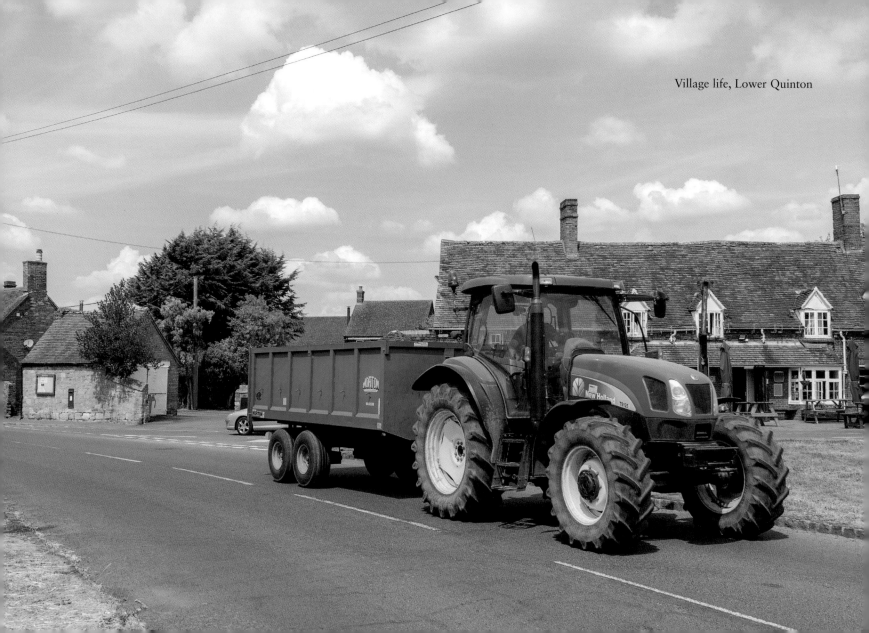

Village life, Lower Quinton

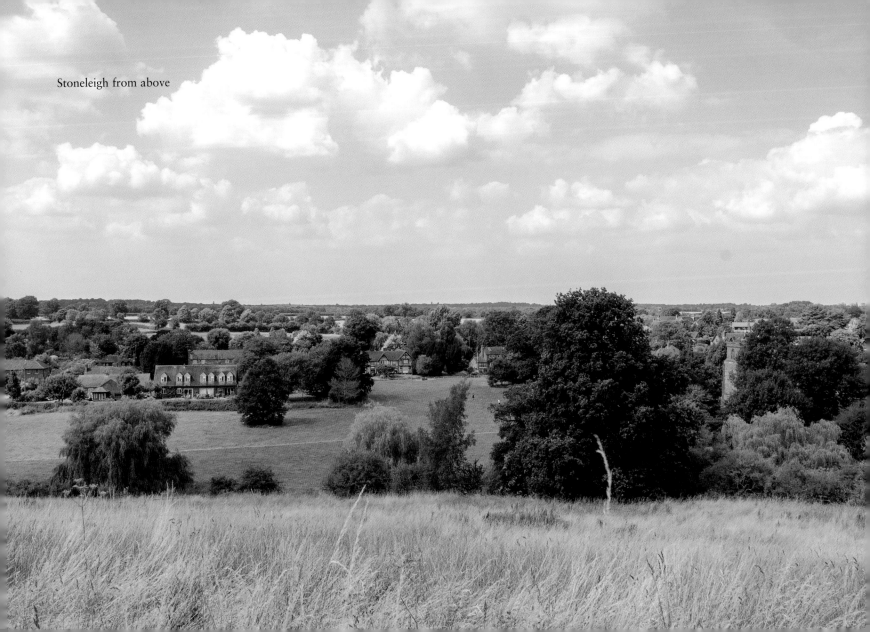
Stoneleigh from above

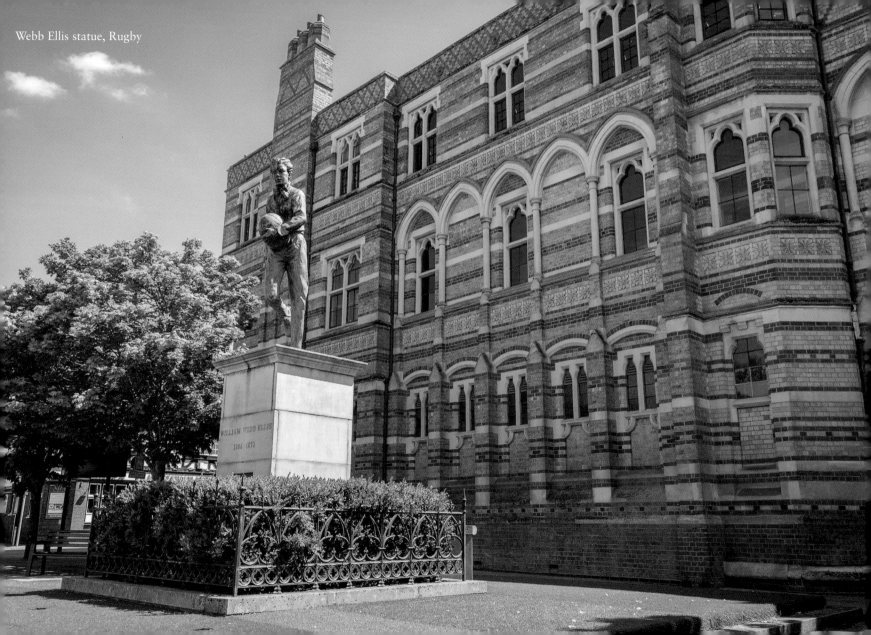
Webb Ellis statue, Rugby

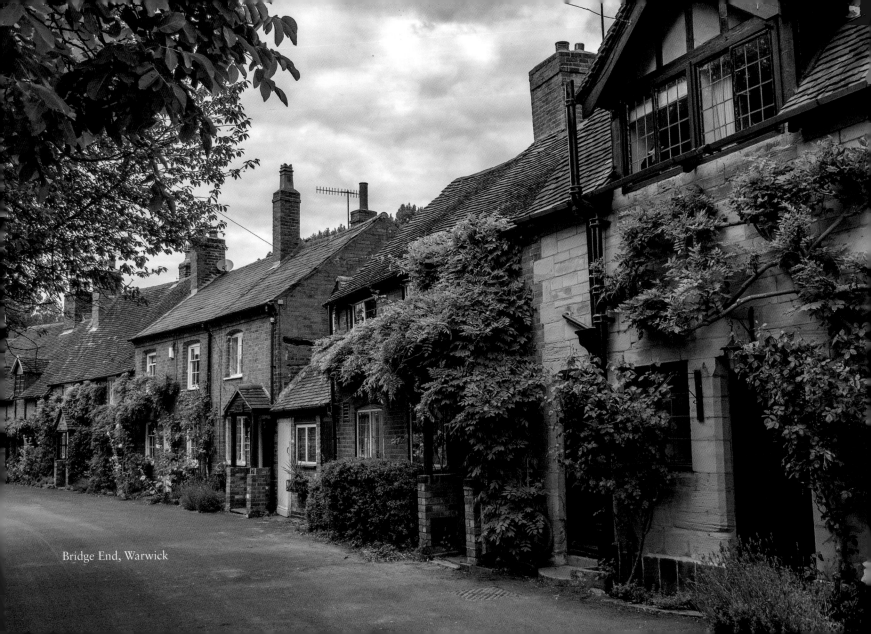

Bridge End, Warwick

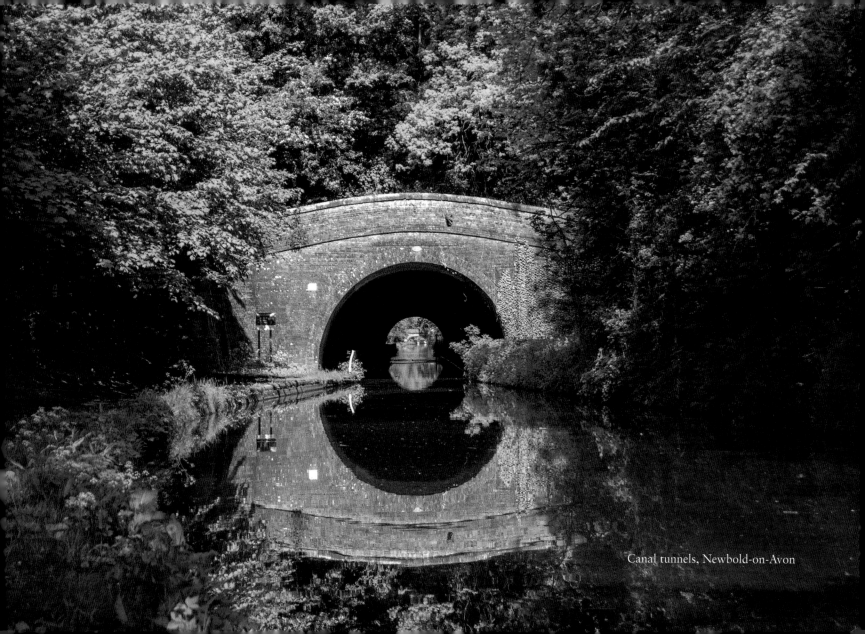

Canal tunnels, Newbold-on-Avon

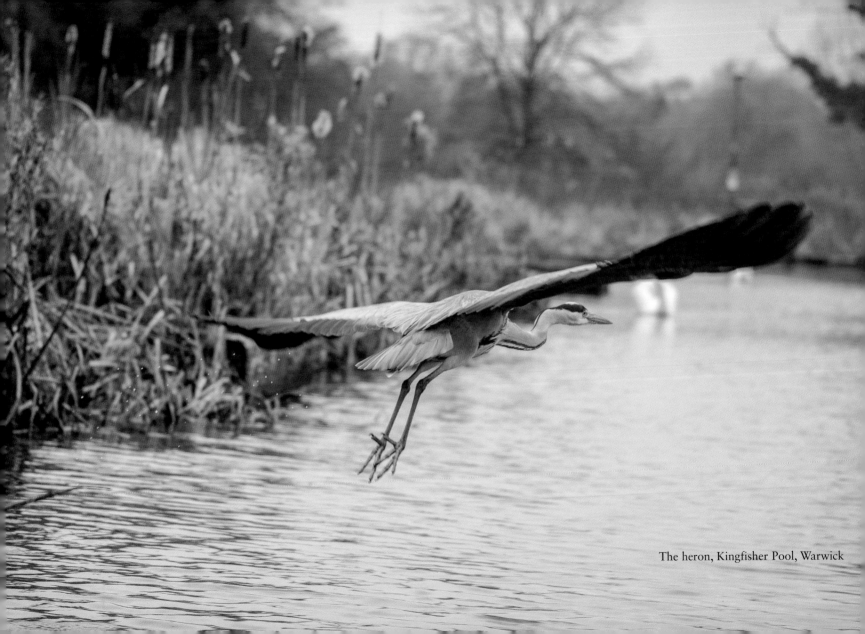

The heron, Kingfisher Pool, Warwick

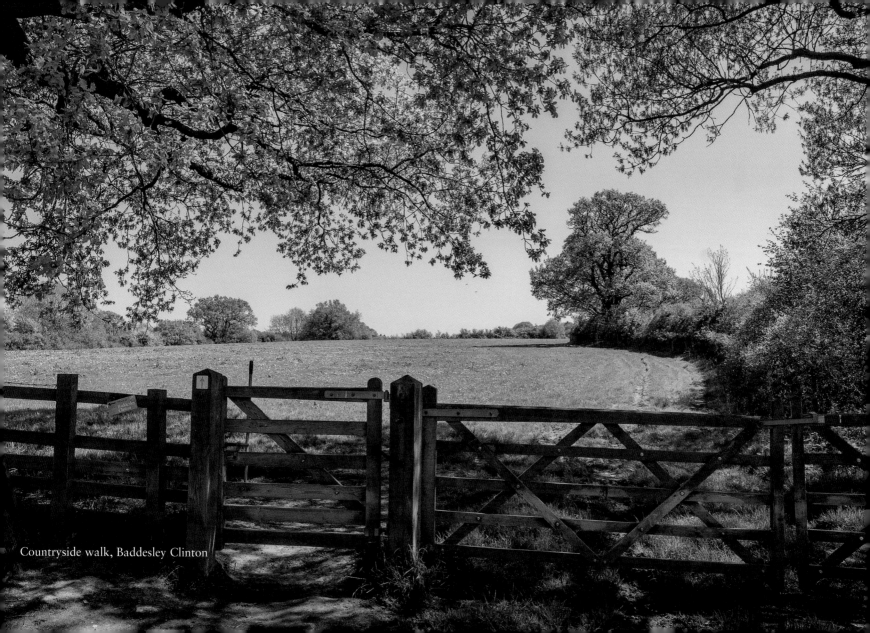

Countryside walk, Baddesley Clinton

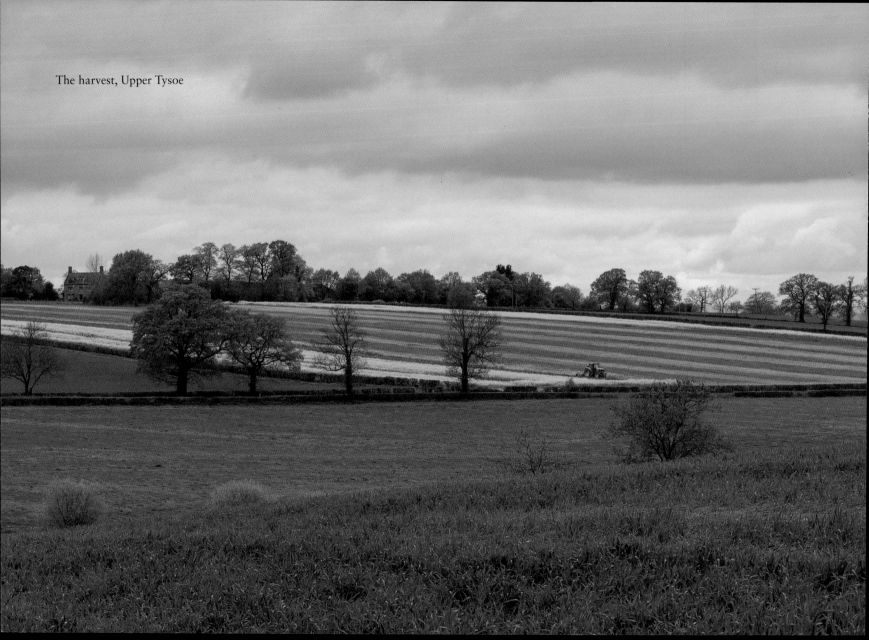

The harvest, Upper Tysoe

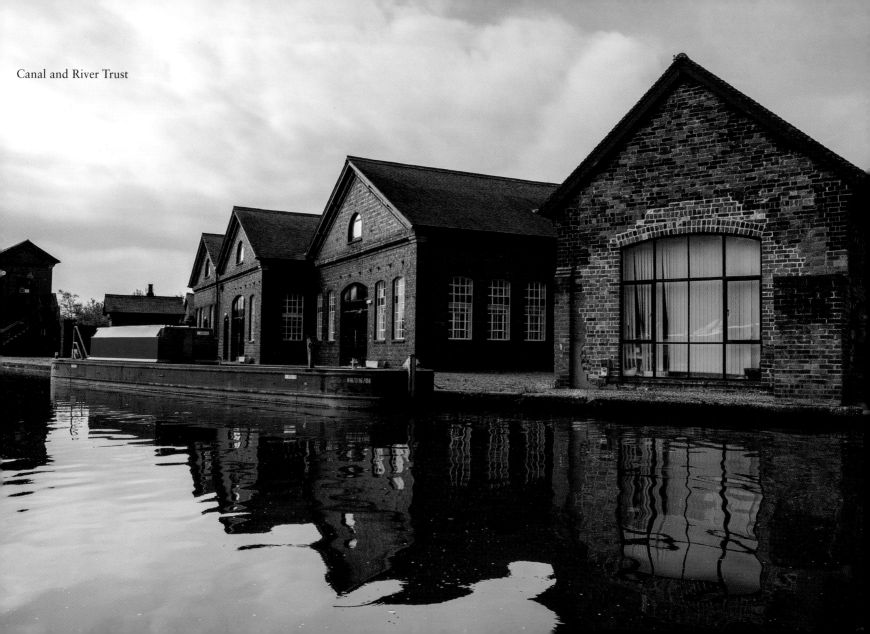

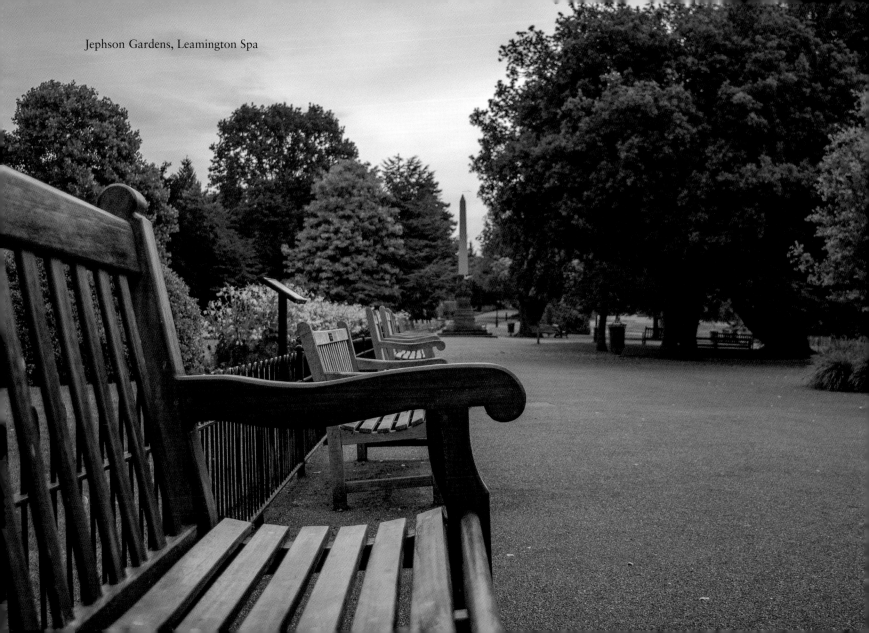

Jephson Gardens, Leamington Spa

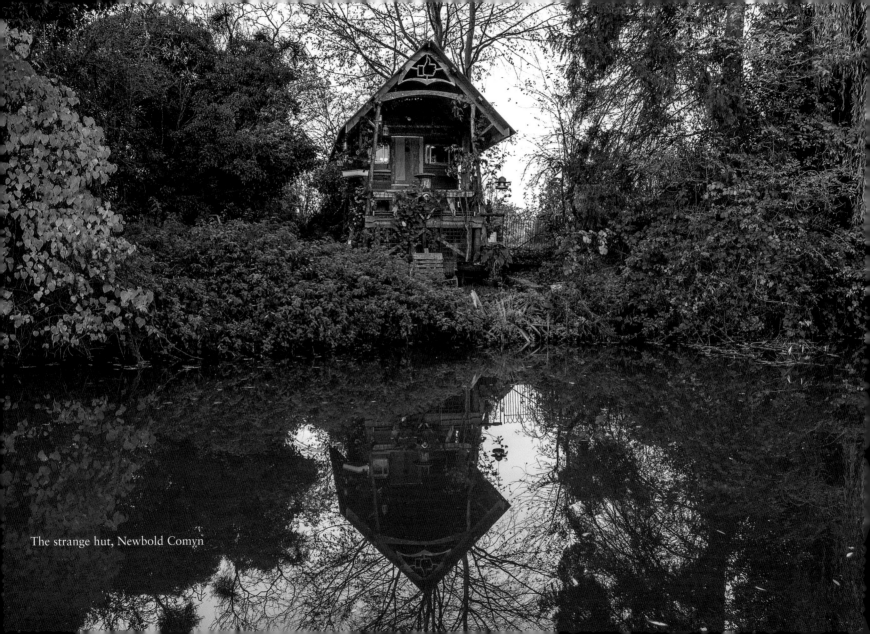

The strange hut, Newbold Comyn

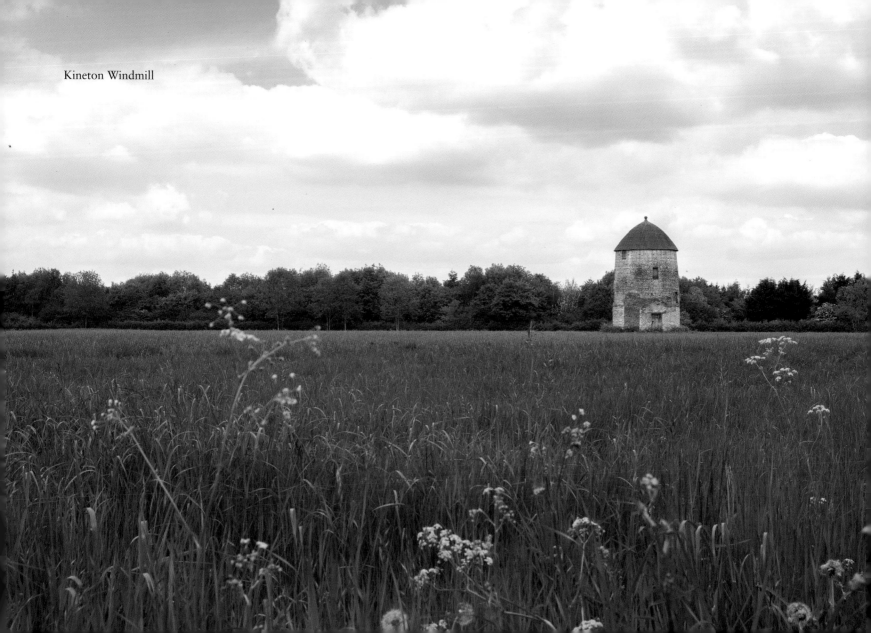

Kineton Windmill

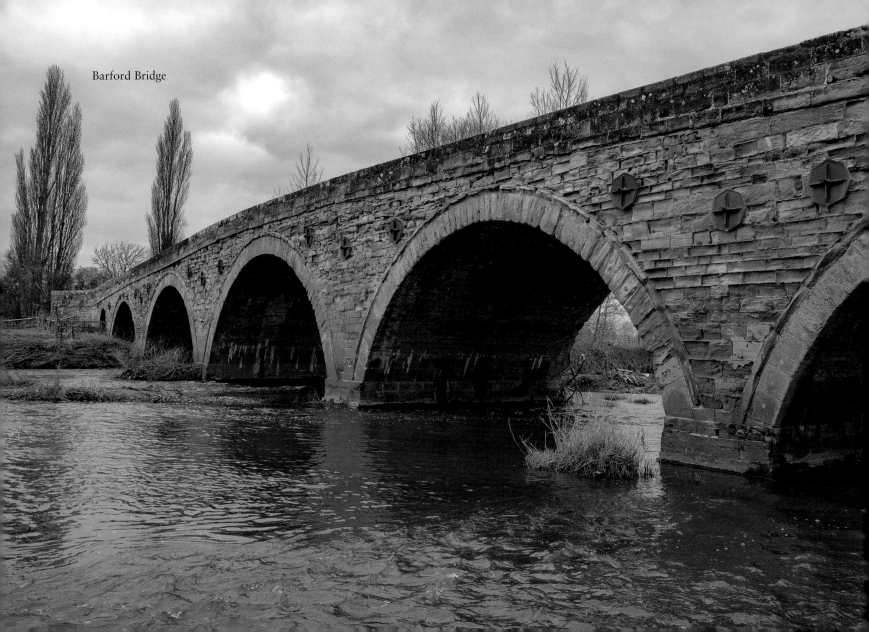

Barford Bridge

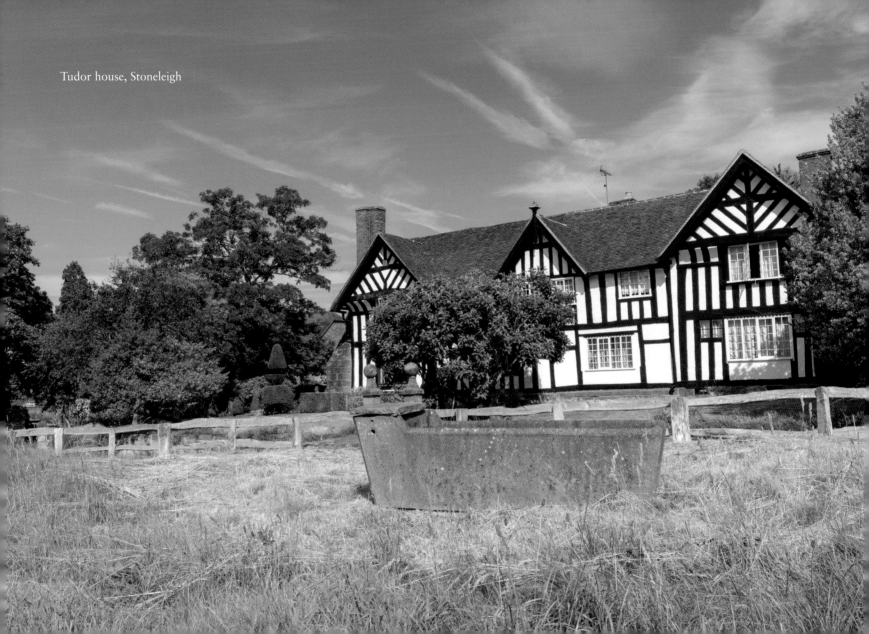
Tudor house, Stoneleigh

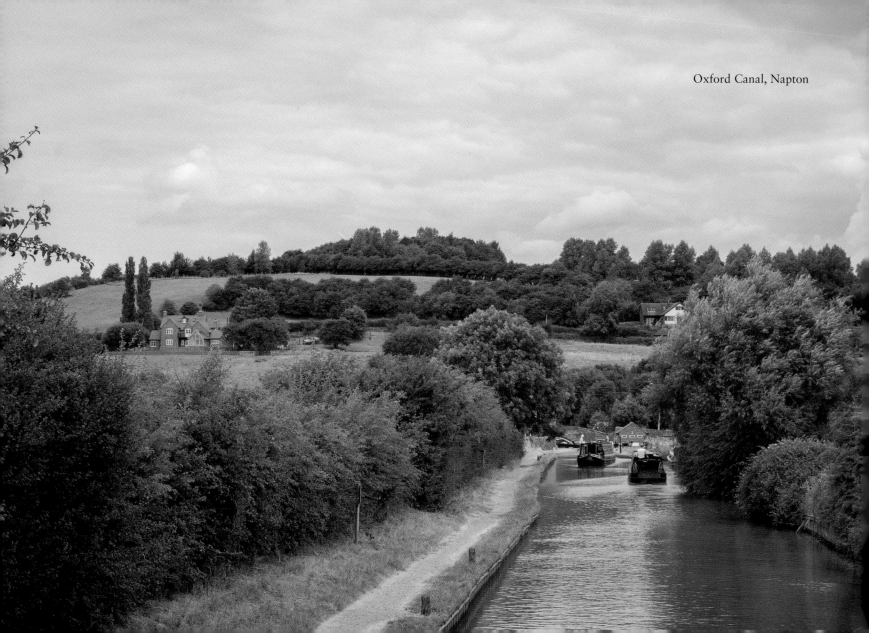

Oxford Canal, Napton

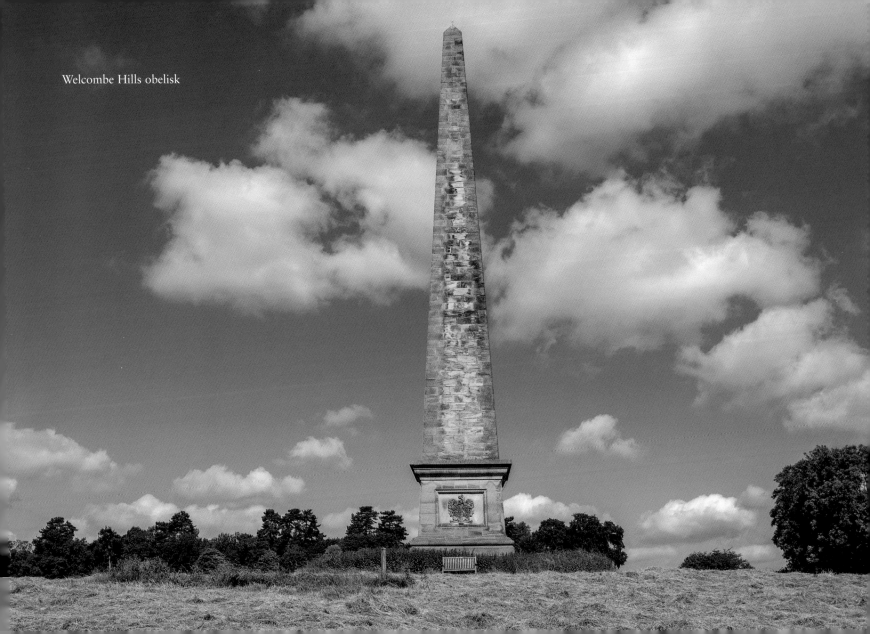

Welcombe Hills obelisk

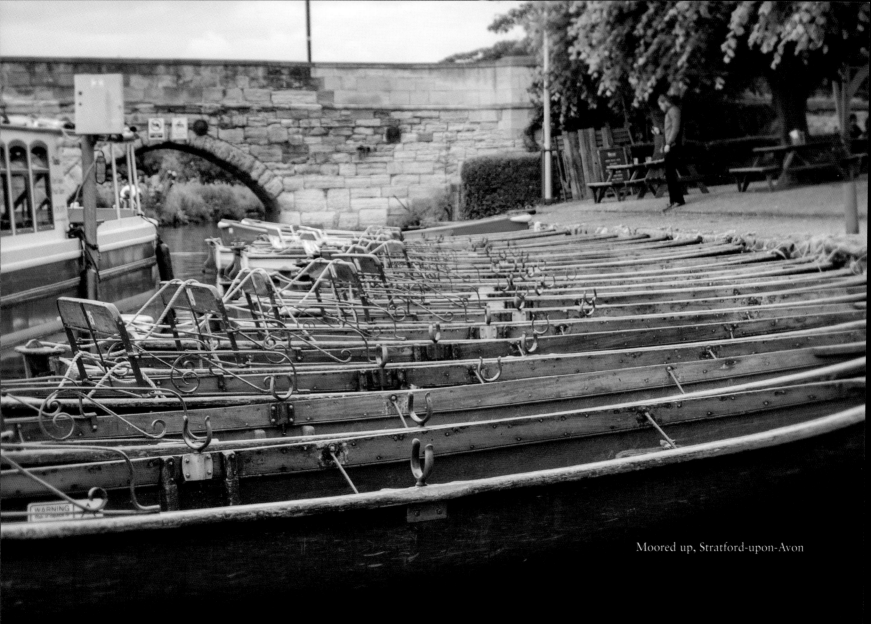

Moored up, Stratford-upon-Avon

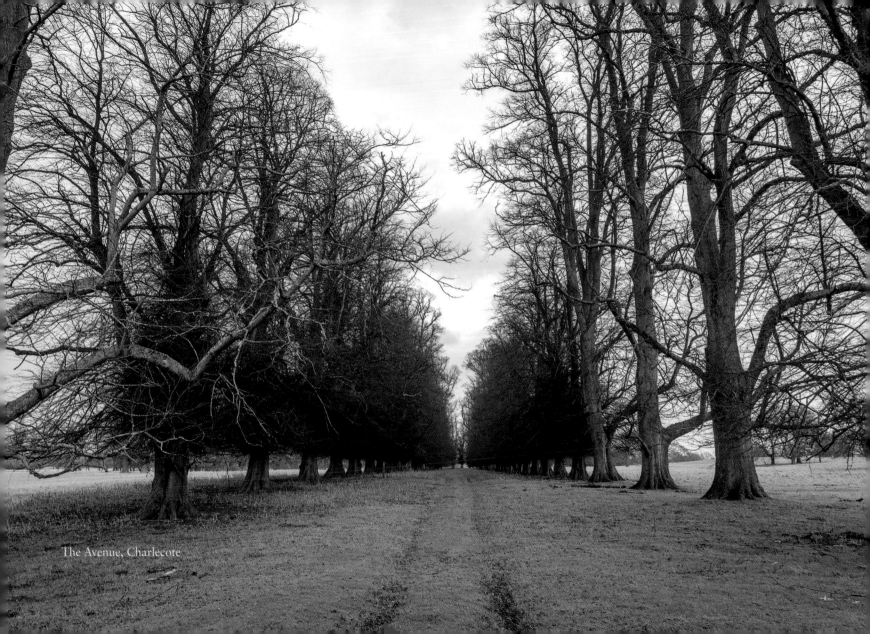

The Avenue, Charlecote

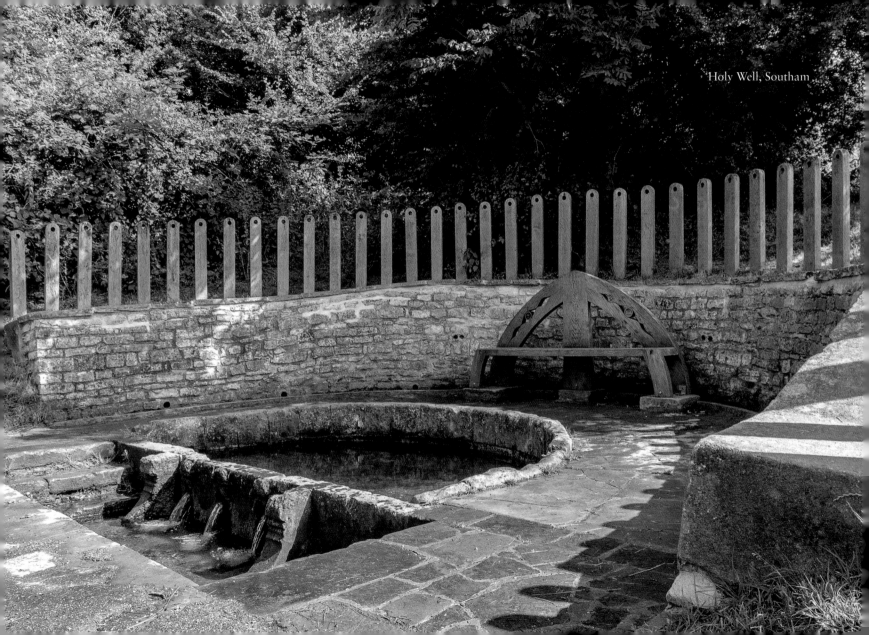

Holy Well, Southam

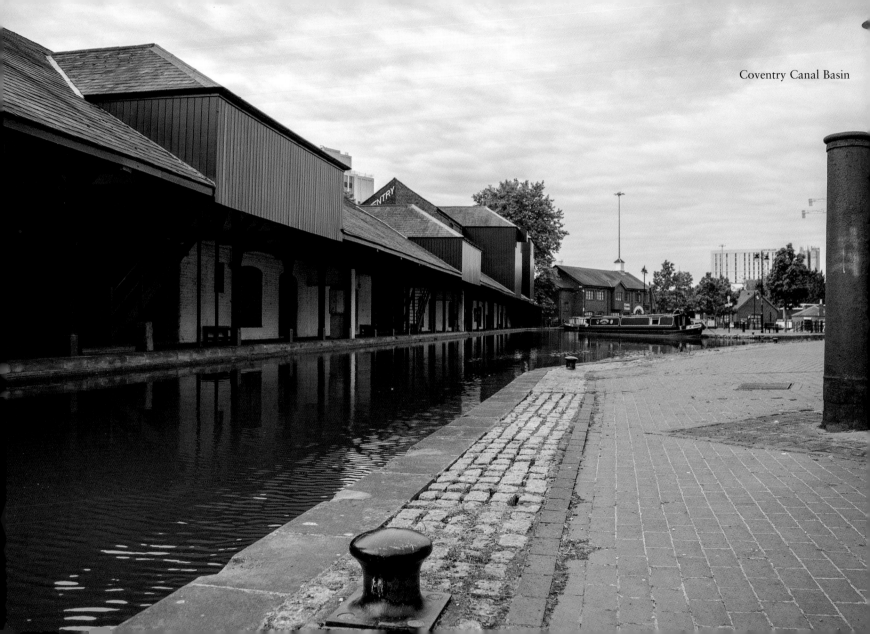

Coventry Canal Basin

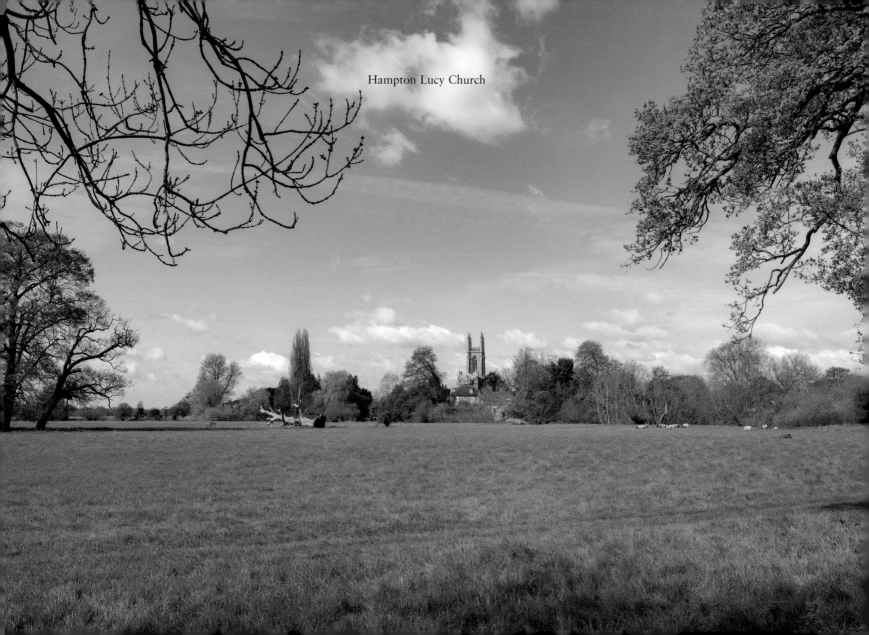

Hampton Lucy Church

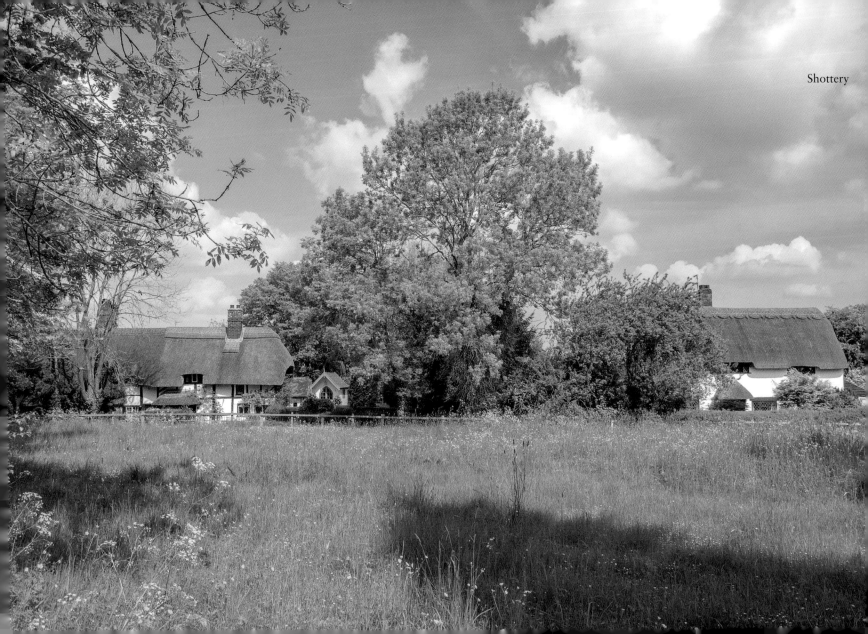

Shottery

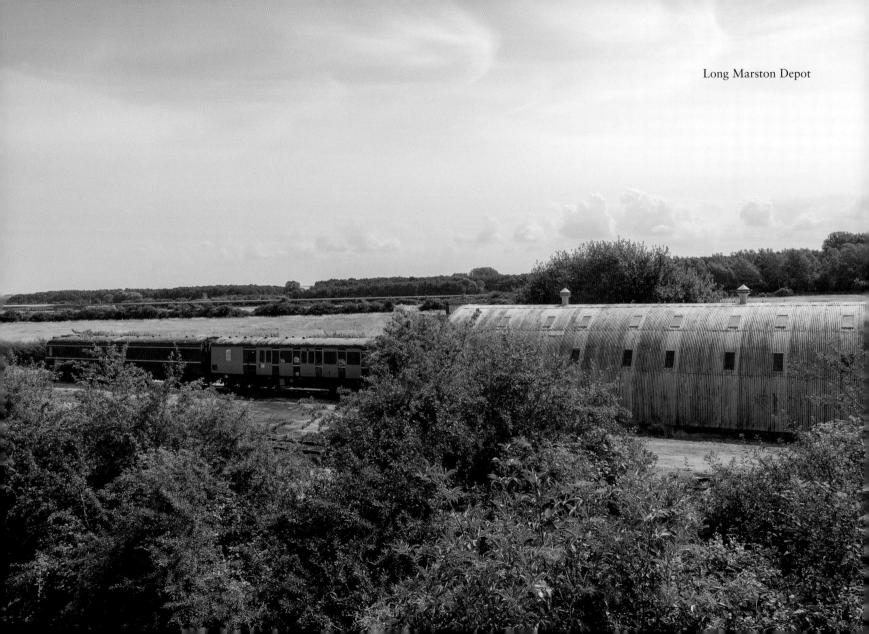

Long Marston Depot

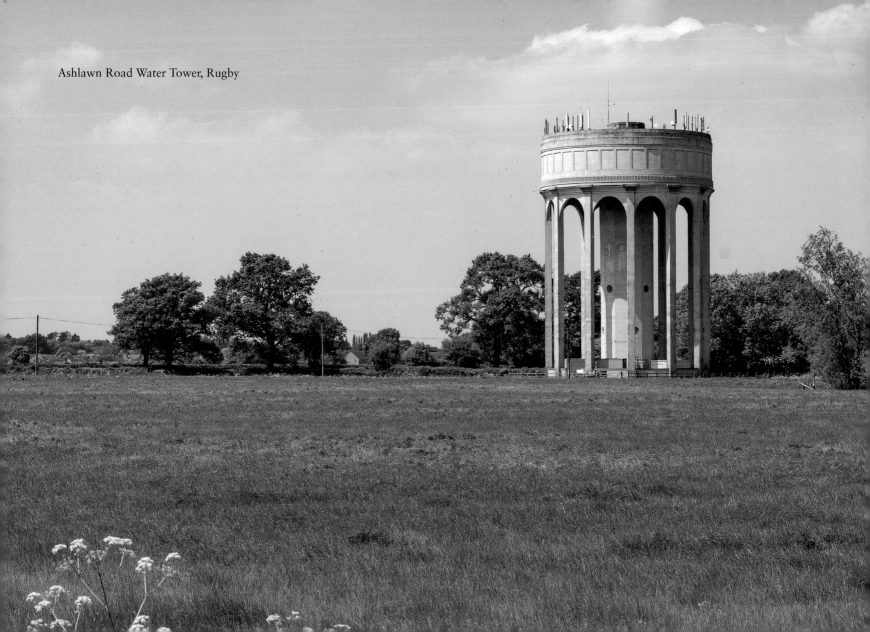

Ashlawn Road Water Tower, Rugby

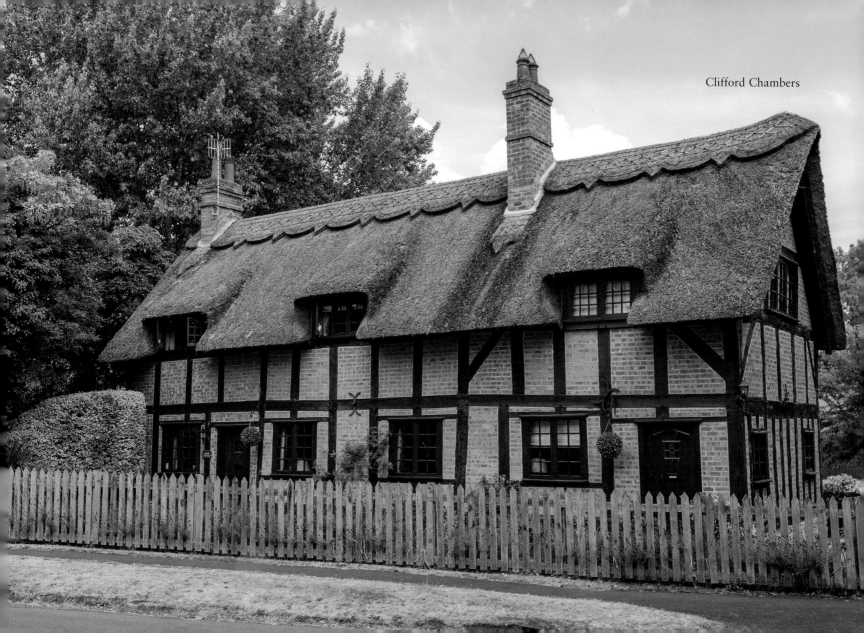

Clifford Chambers

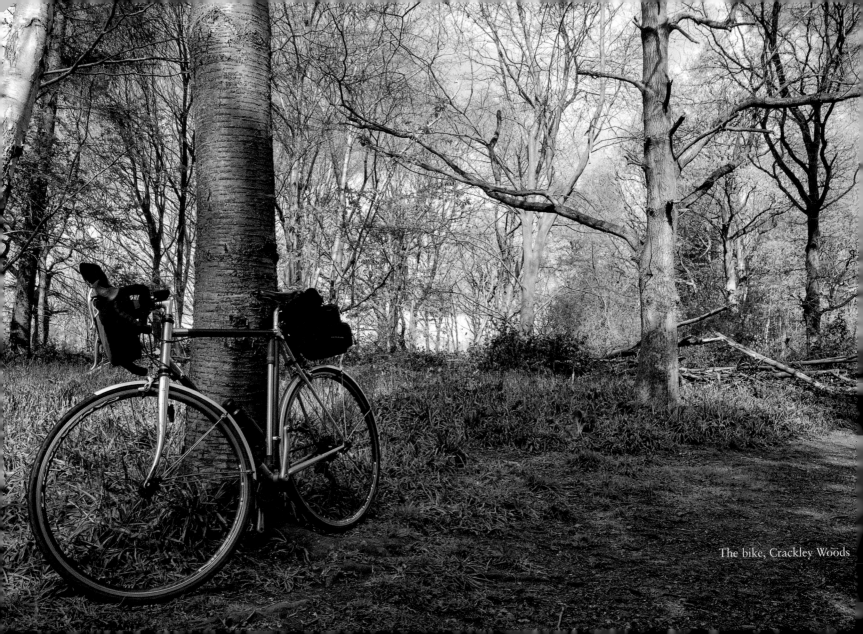

The bike, Crackley Woods

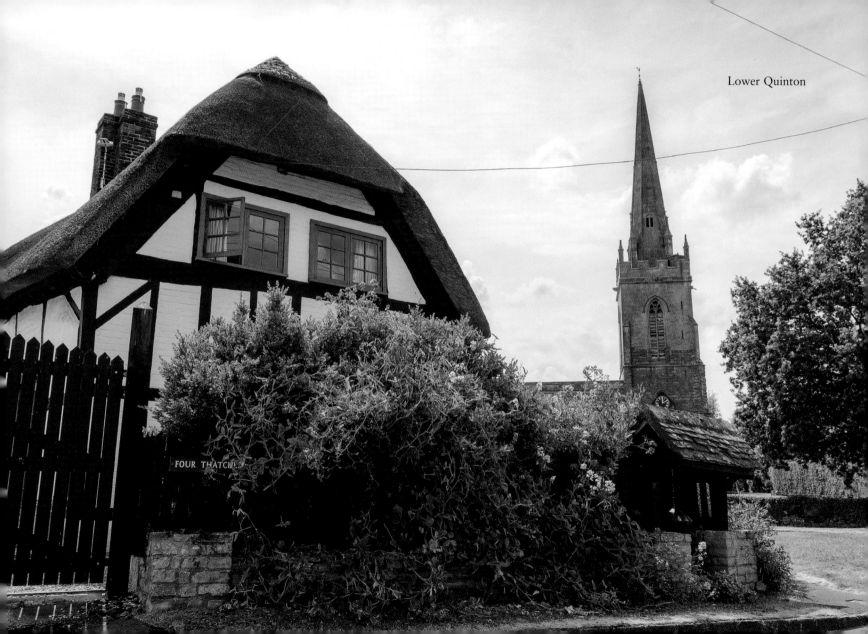

Lower Quinton

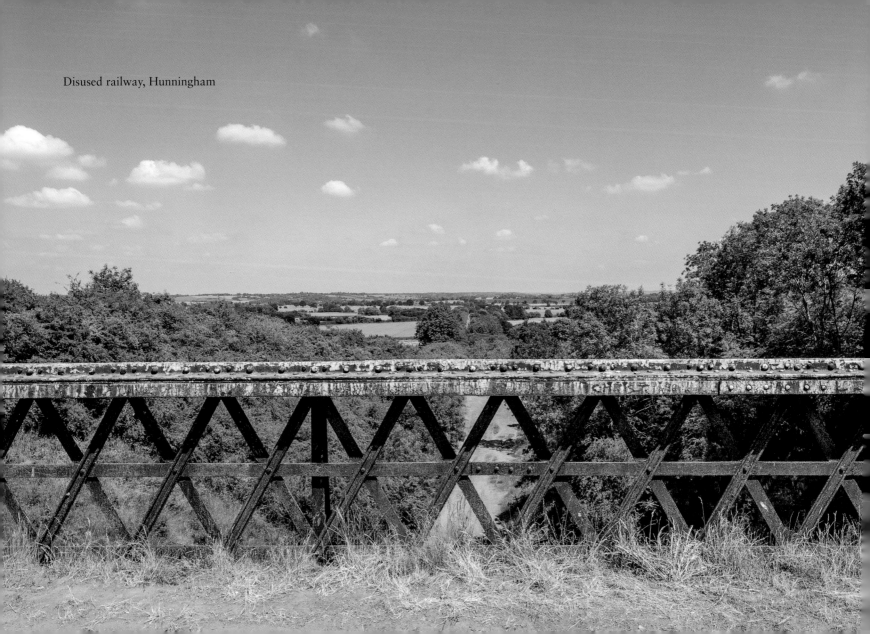

Disused railway, Hunningham

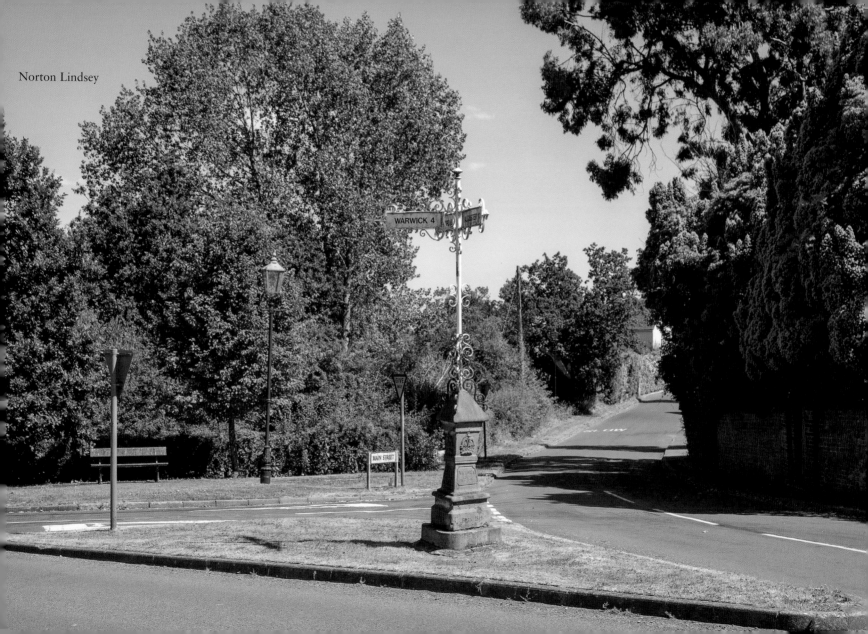

Norton Lindsey

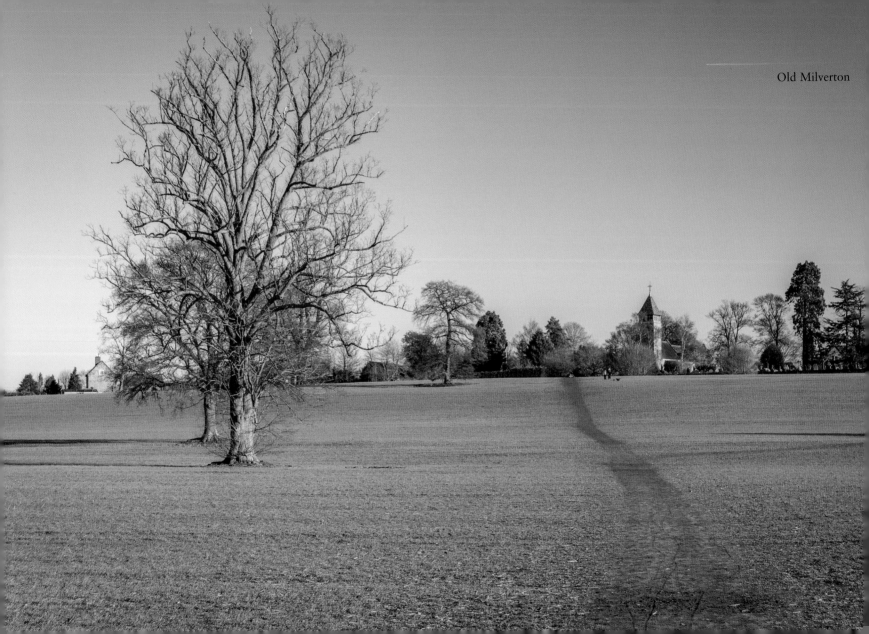

Old Milverton

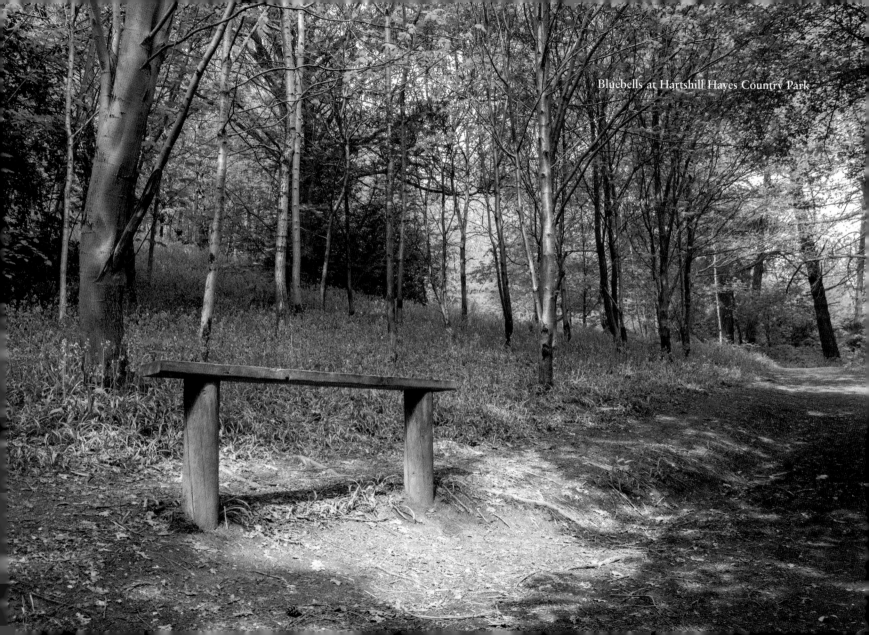
Bluebells at Hartshill Hayes Country Park

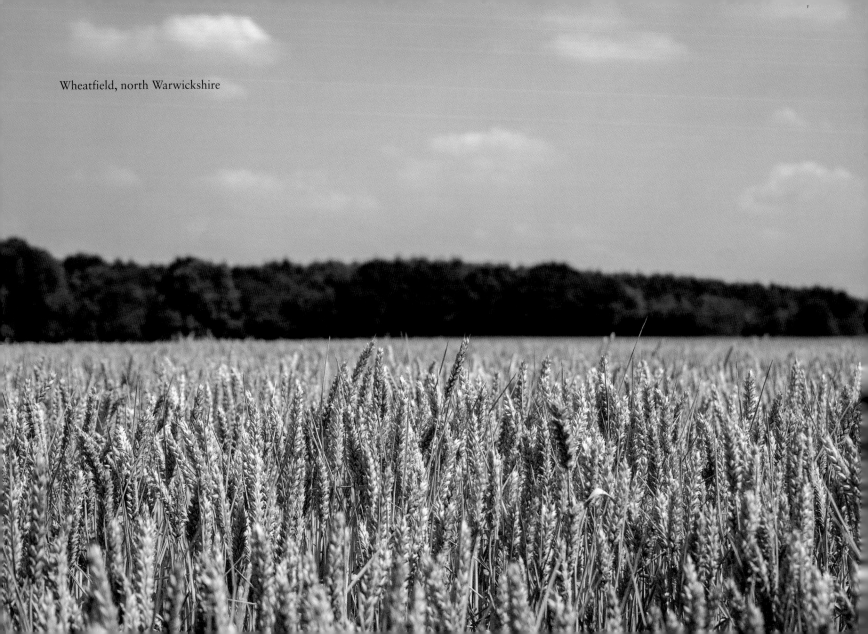

Wheatfield, north Warwickshire

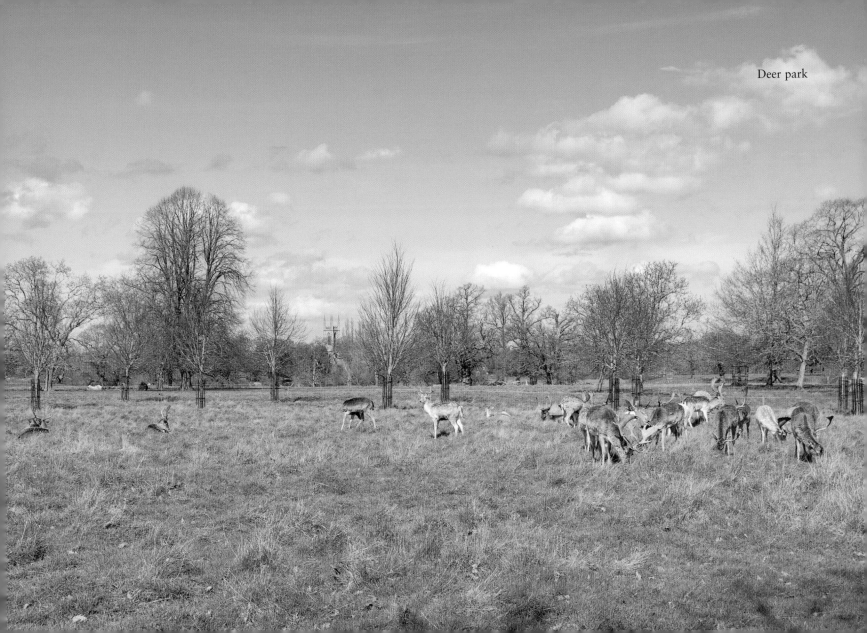

Deer park

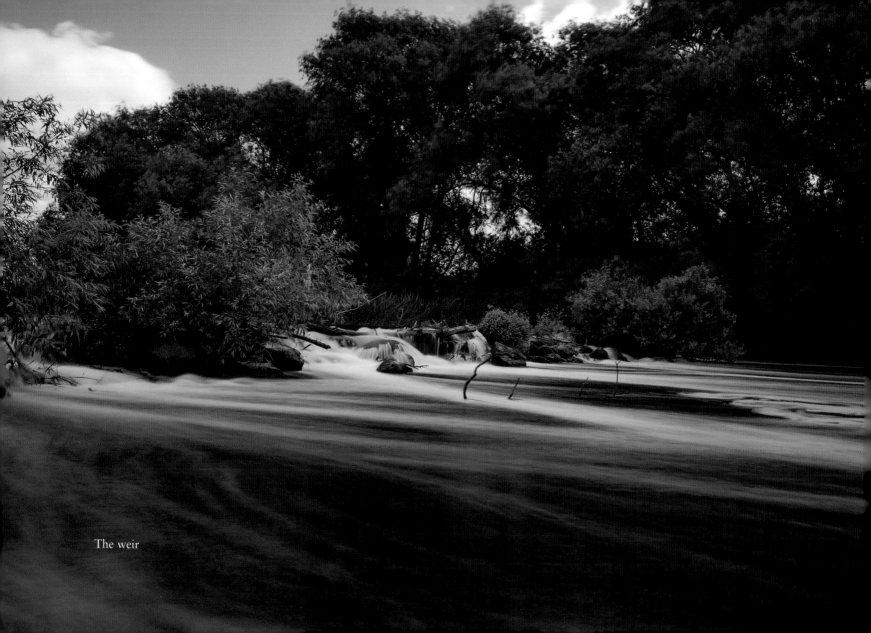

The weir

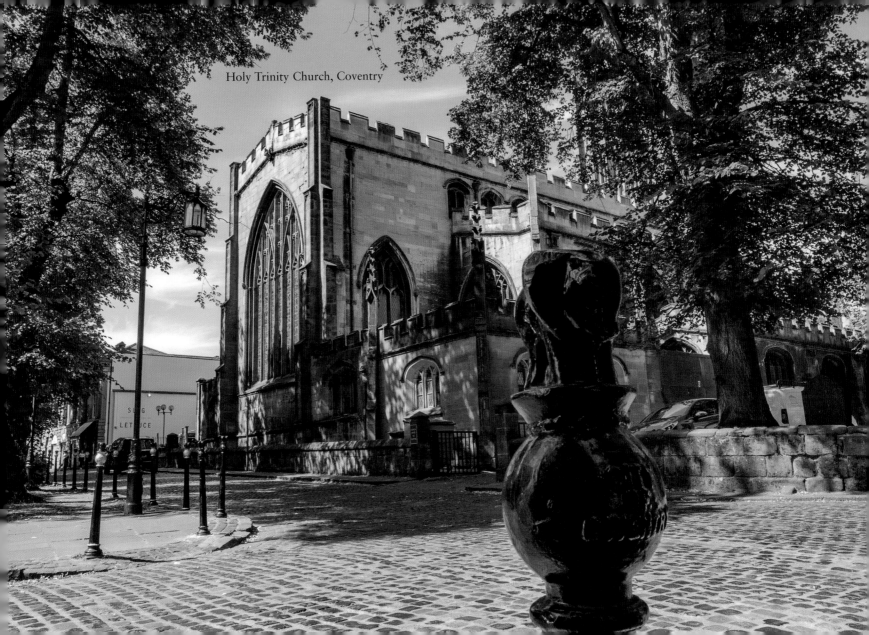

Holy Trinity Church, Coventry

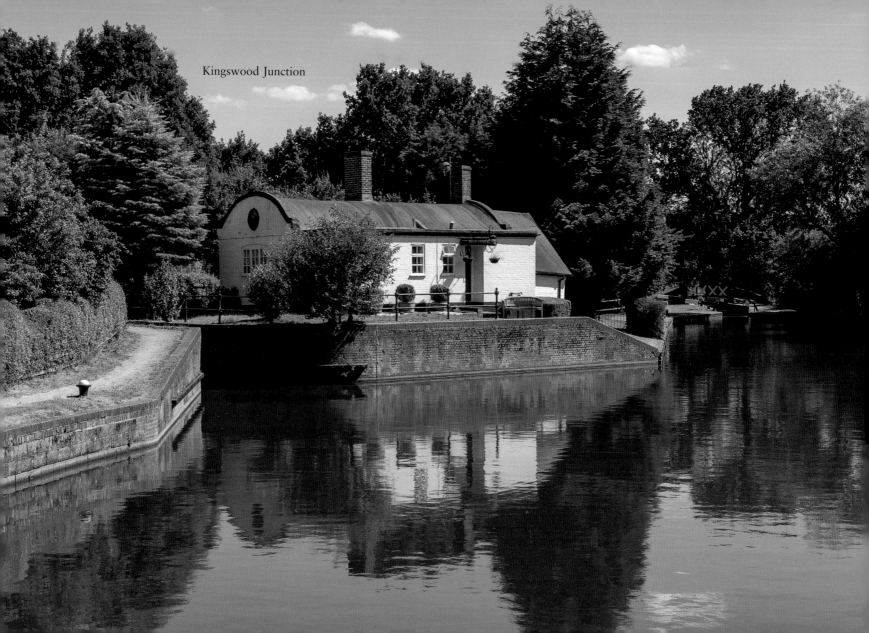

Kingswood Junction

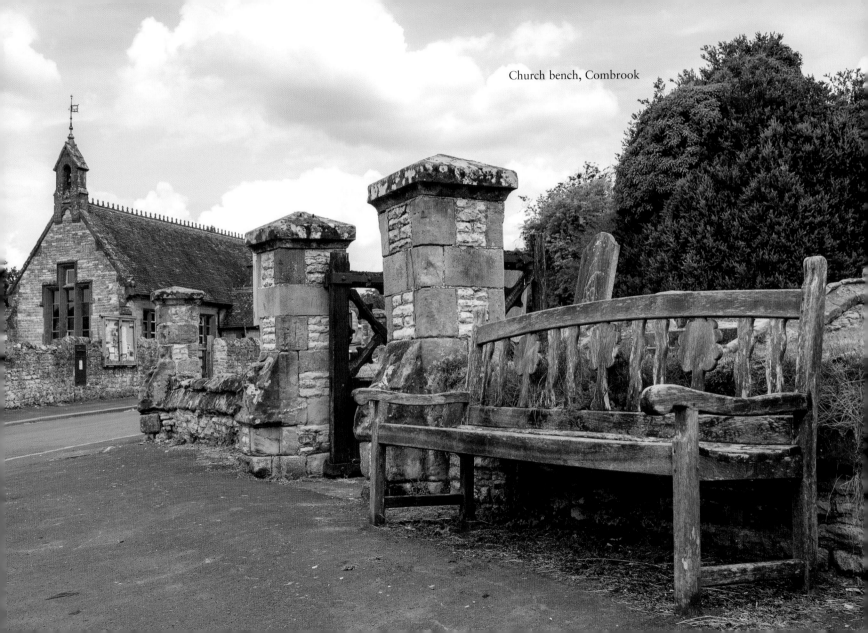

Church bench, Combrook

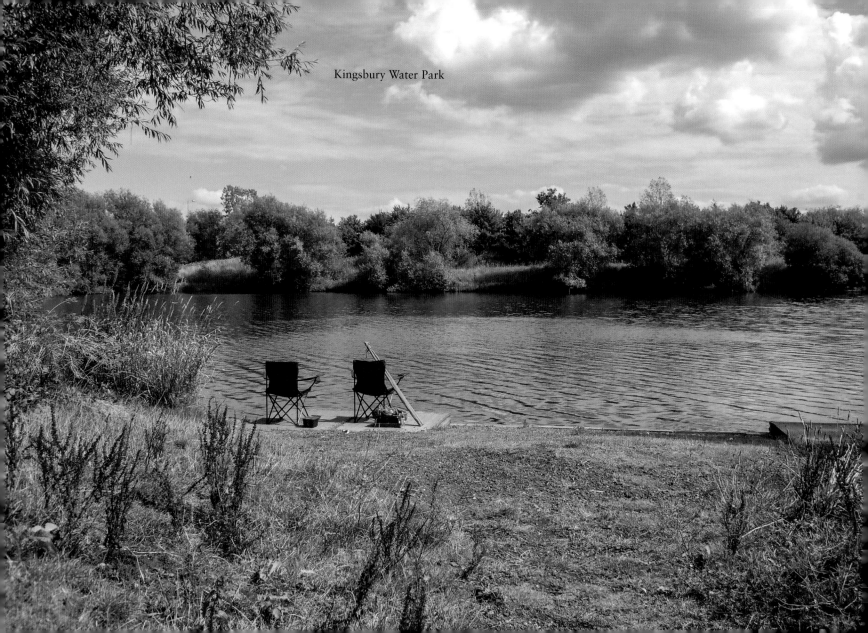

Kingsbury Water Park

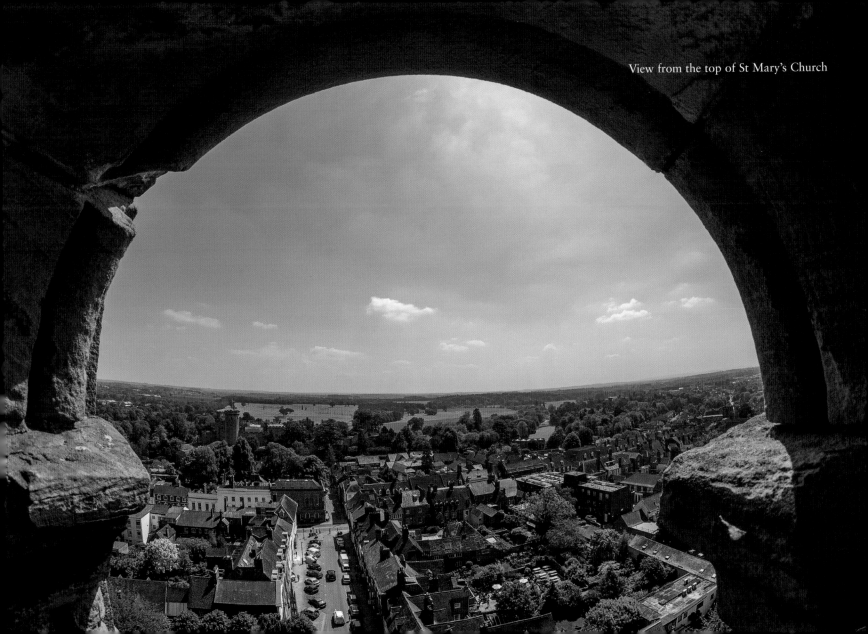

View from the top of St Mary's Church

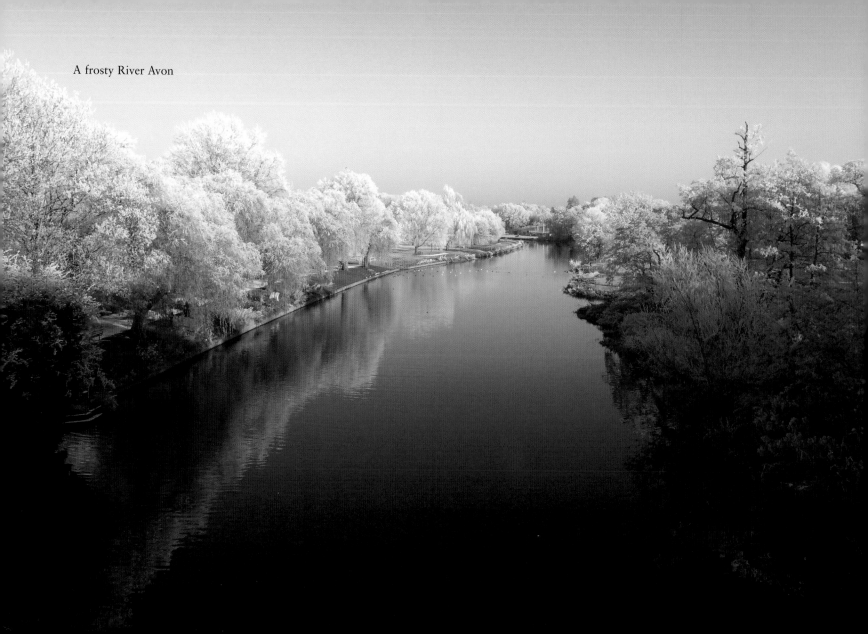

A frosty River Avon

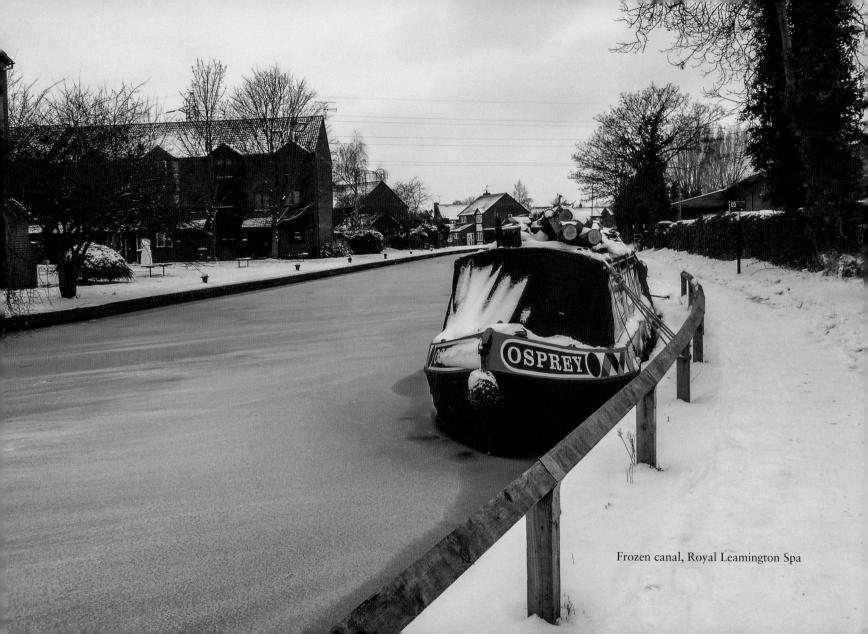

Frozen canal, Royal Leamington Spa

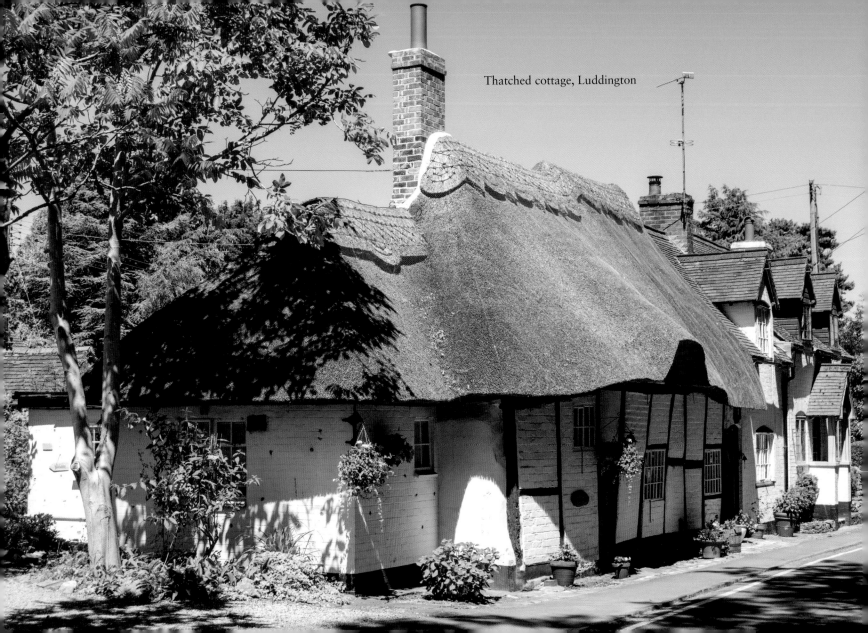

Thatched cottage, Luddington

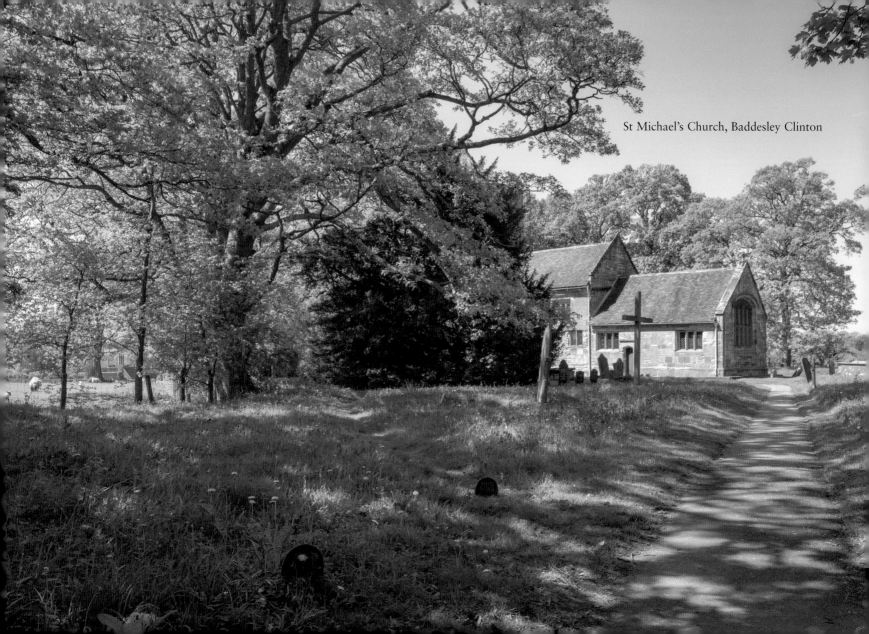
St Michael's Church, Baddesley Clinton

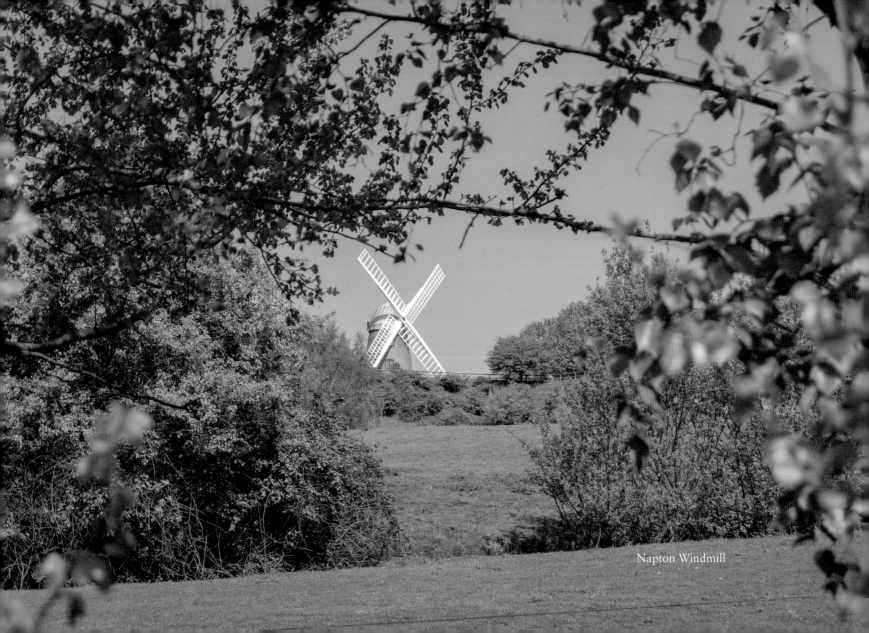

Napton Windmill

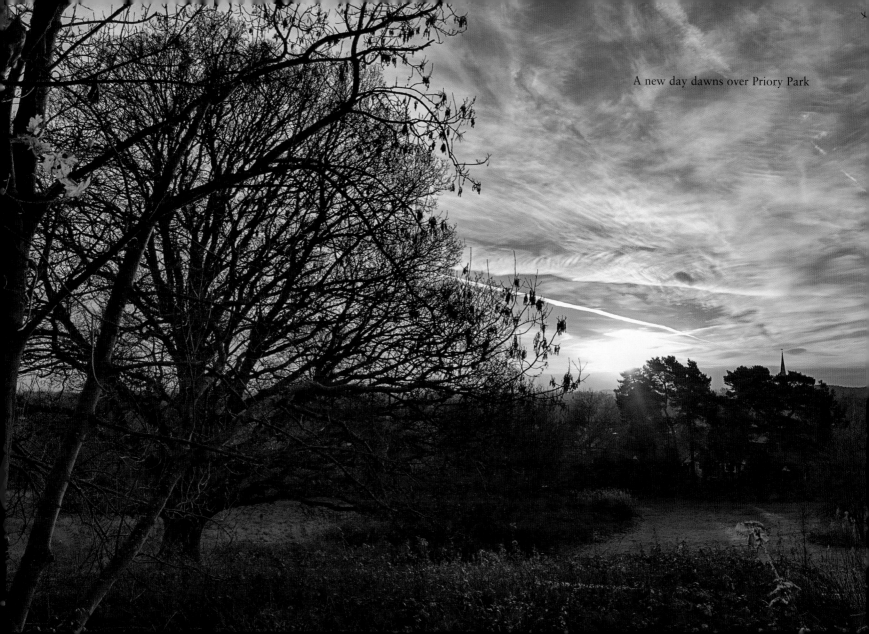

A new day dawns over Priory Park

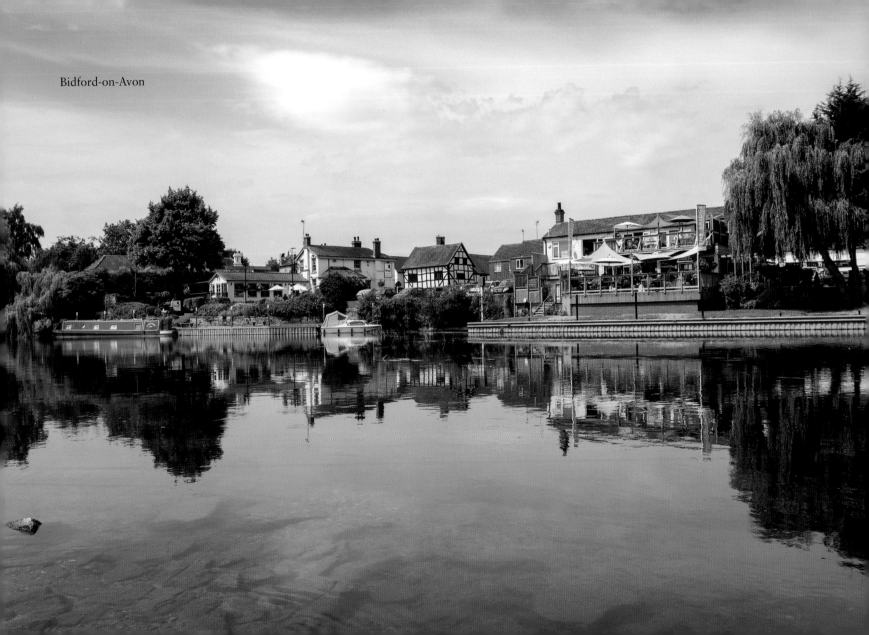

Bidford-on-Avon

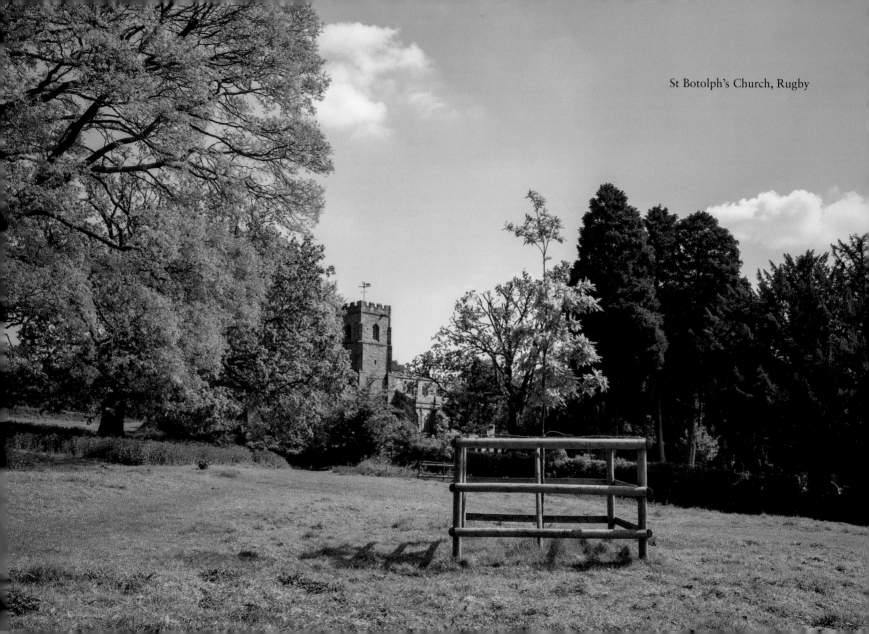

St Botolph's Church, Rugby

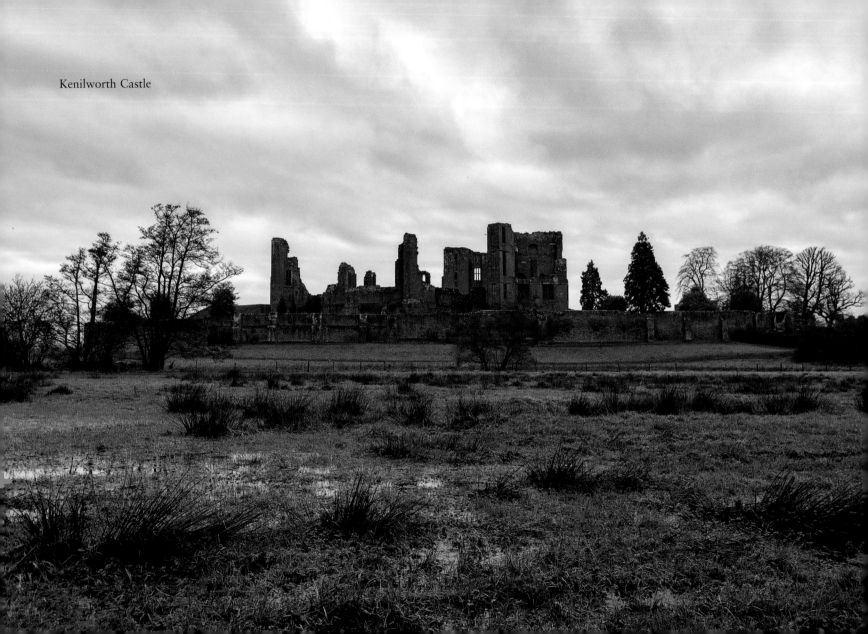

Kenilworth Castle

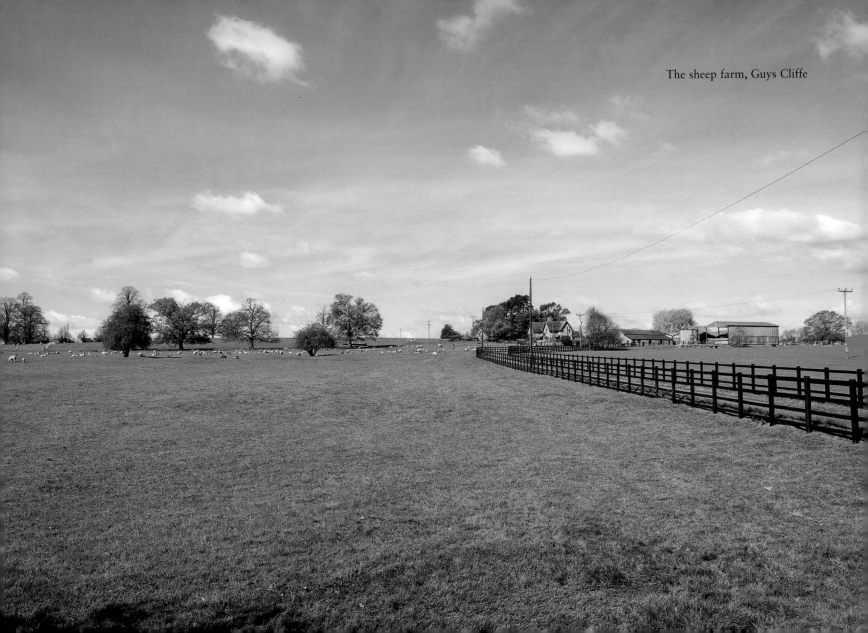

The sheep farm, Guys Cliffe

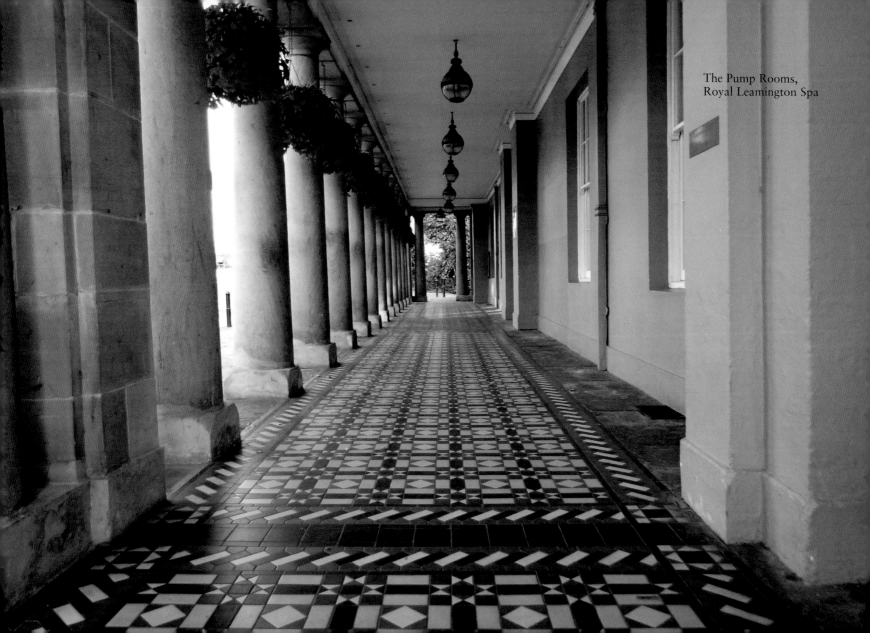

The Pump Rooms,
Royal Leamington Spa

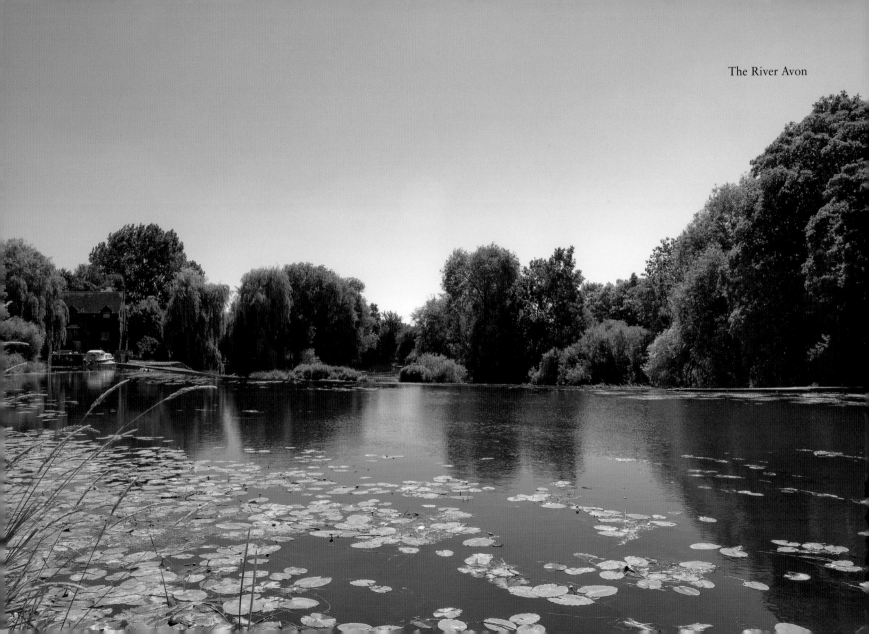

The River Avon

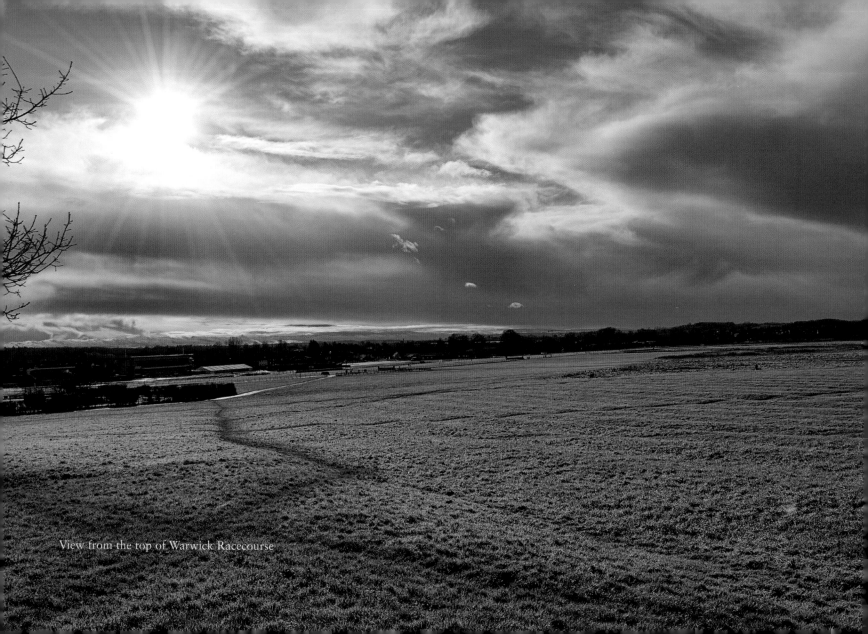

View from the top of Warwick Racecourse

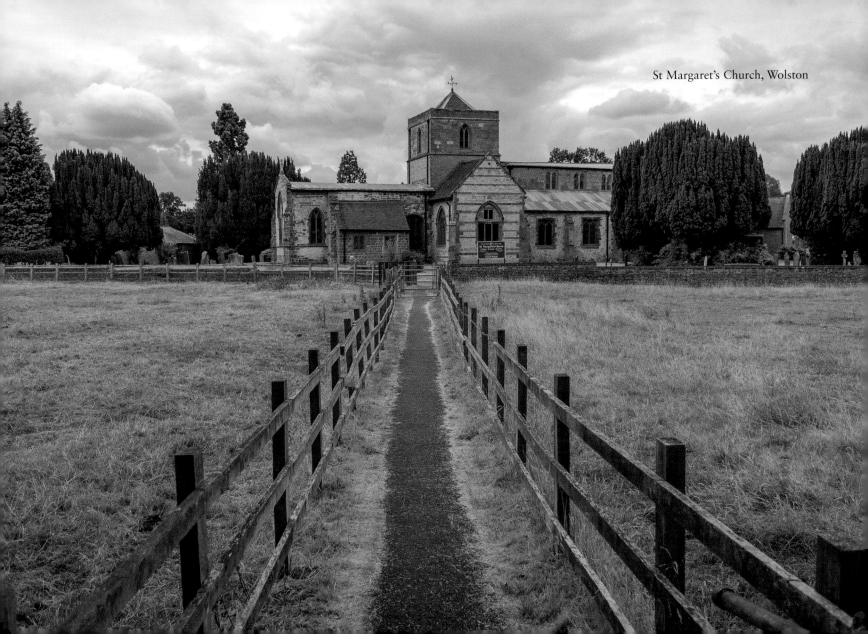

St Margaret's Church, Wolston

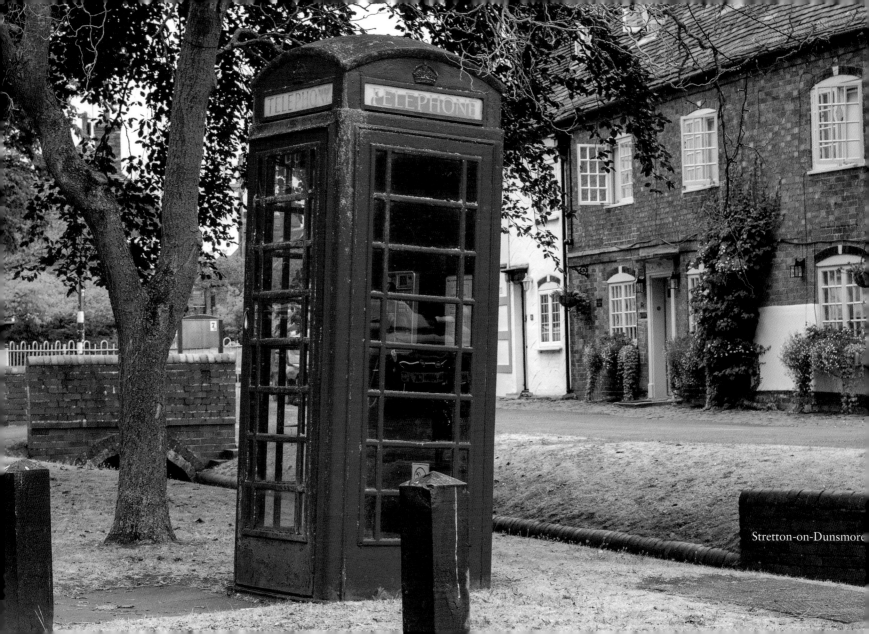

Stretton-on-Dunsmore

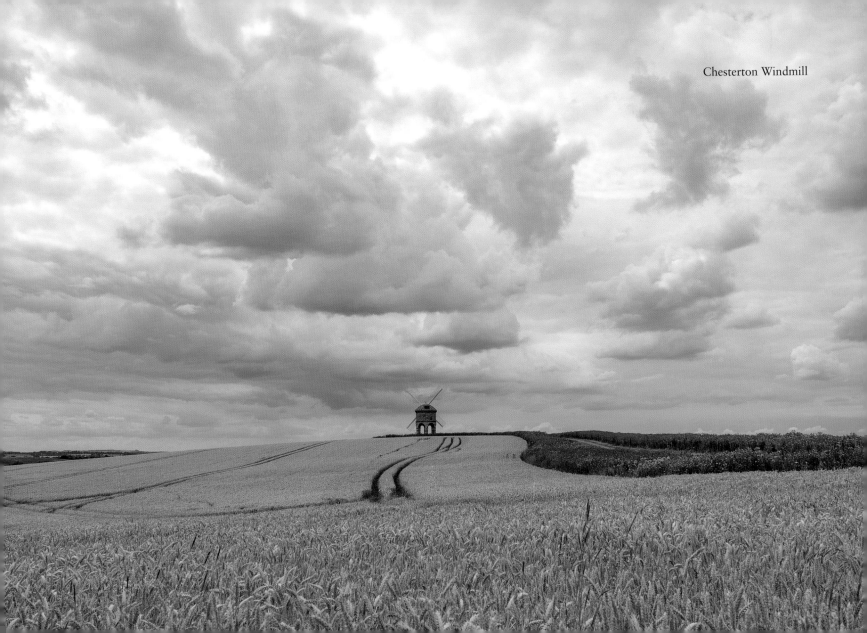

Chesterton Windmill

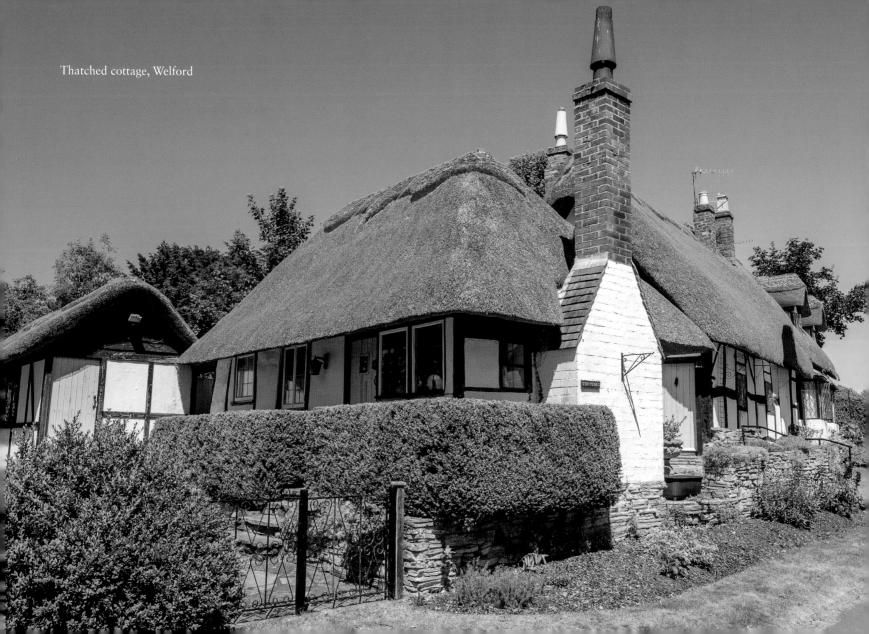

Thatched cottage, Welford

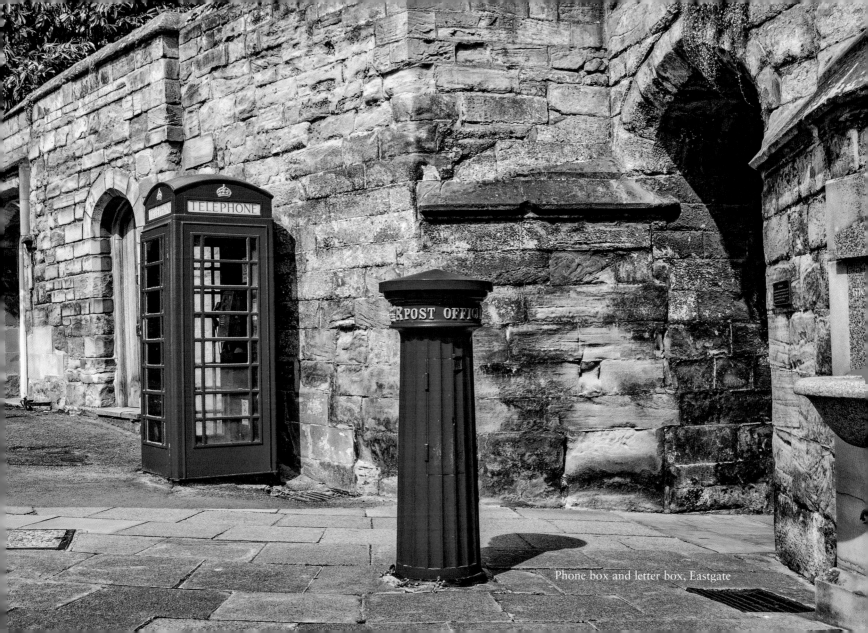

Phone box and letter box, Eastgate

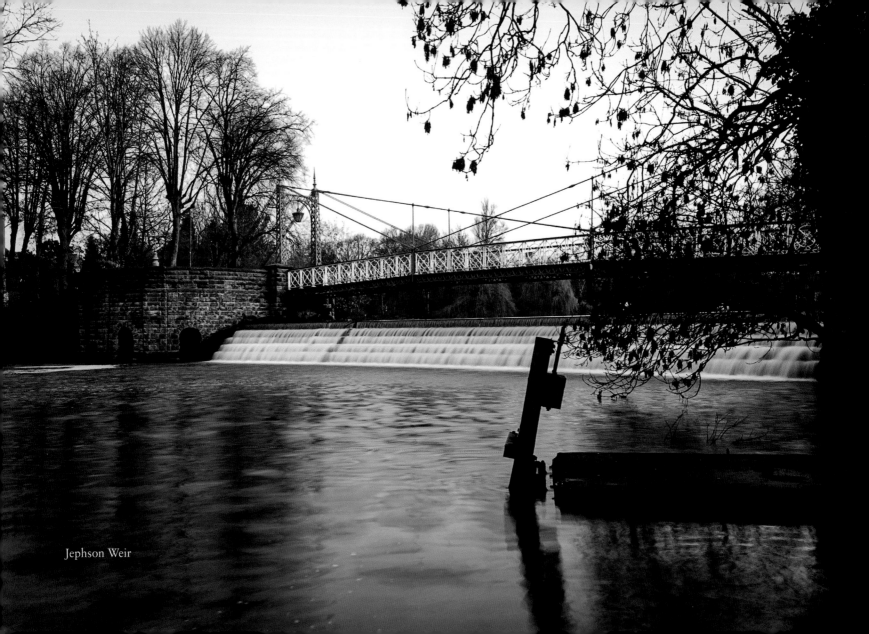

Jephson Weir

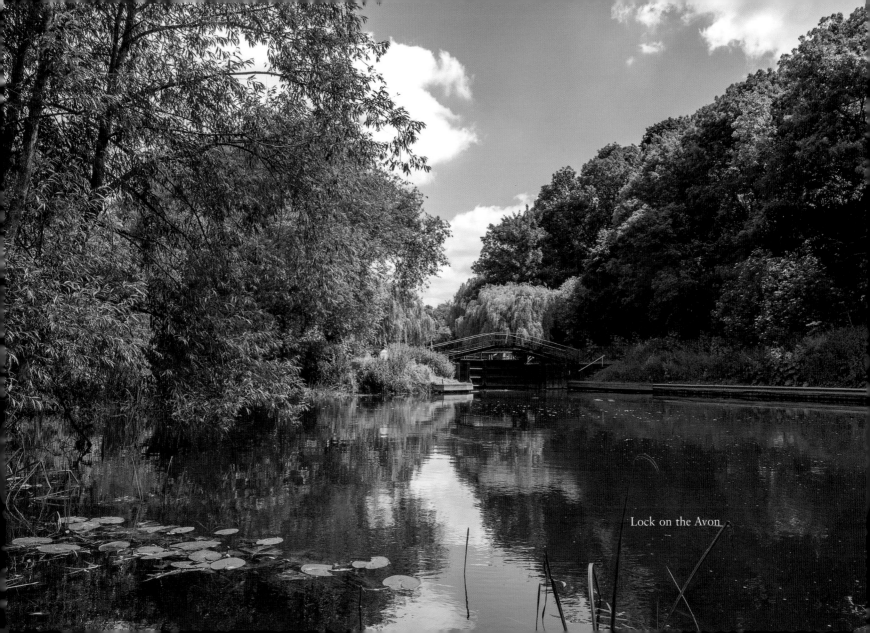

Lock on the Avon

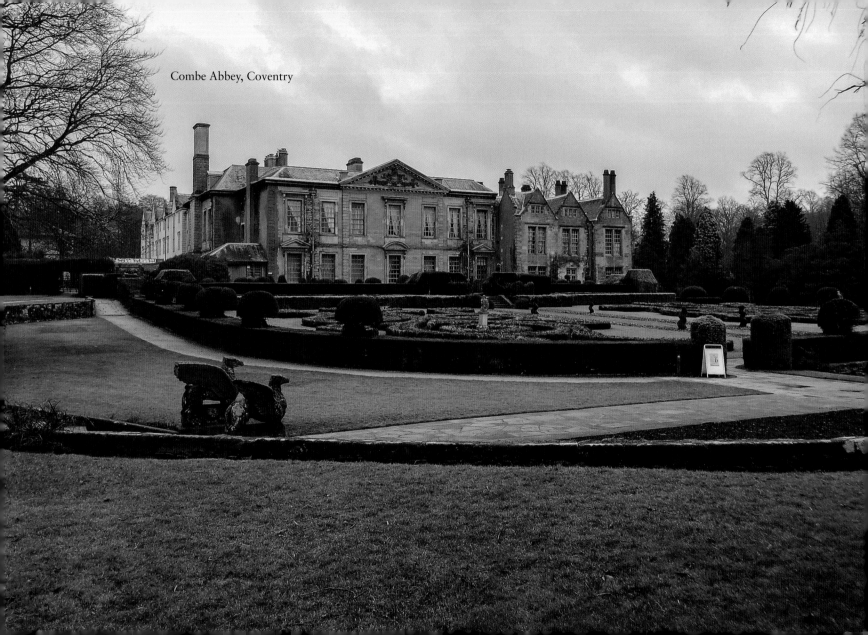

Combe Abbey, Coventry

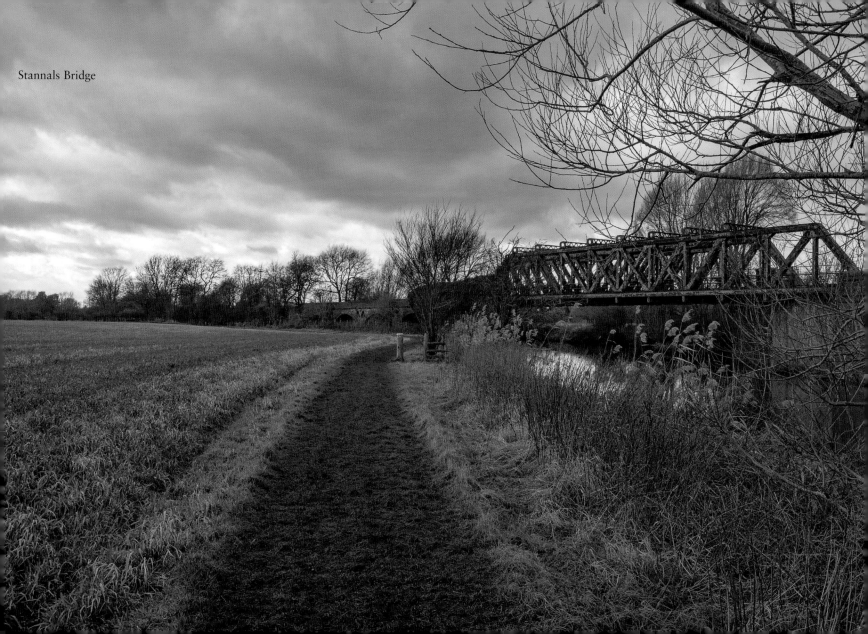

Stannals Bridge

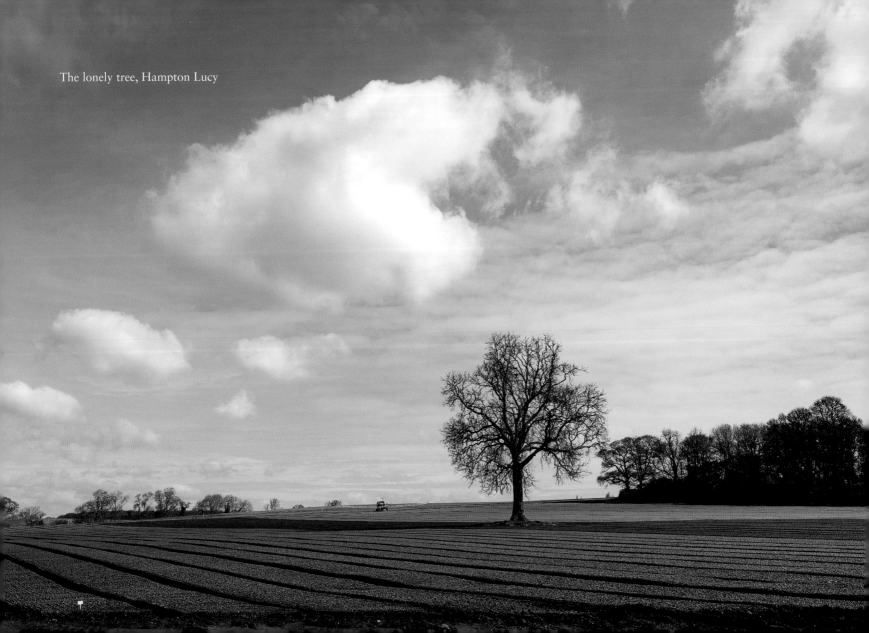

The lonely tree, Hampton Lucy

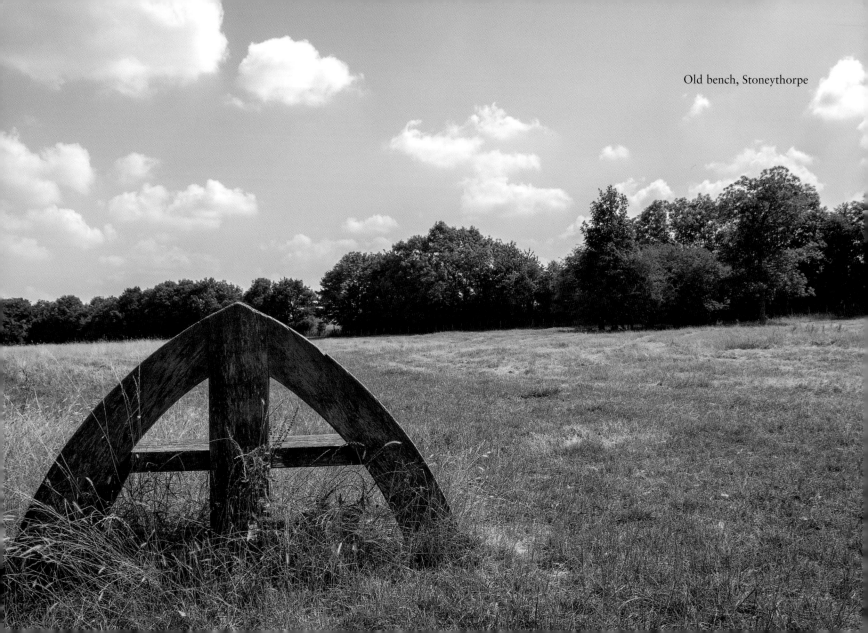

Old bench, Stoneythorpe

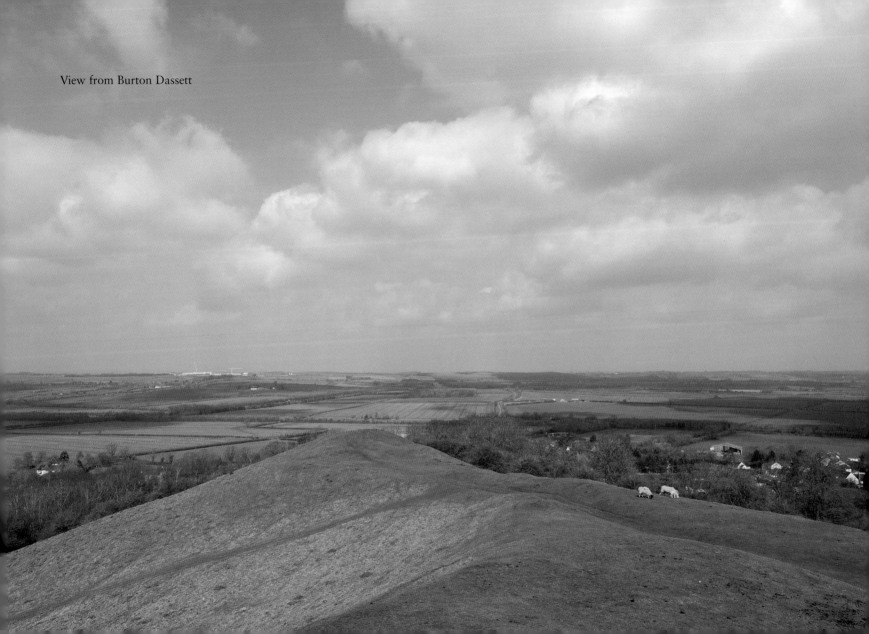

View from Burton Dassett

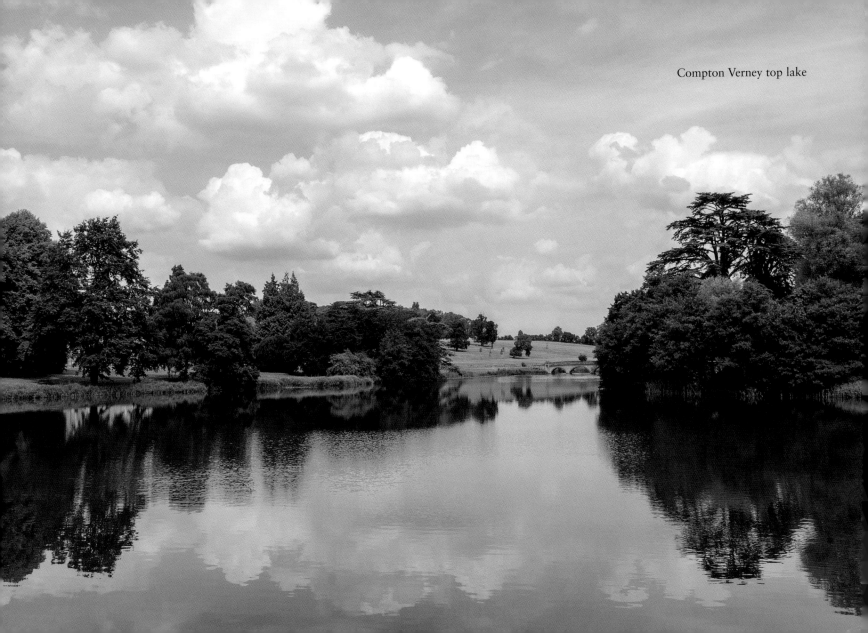

Compton Verney top lake

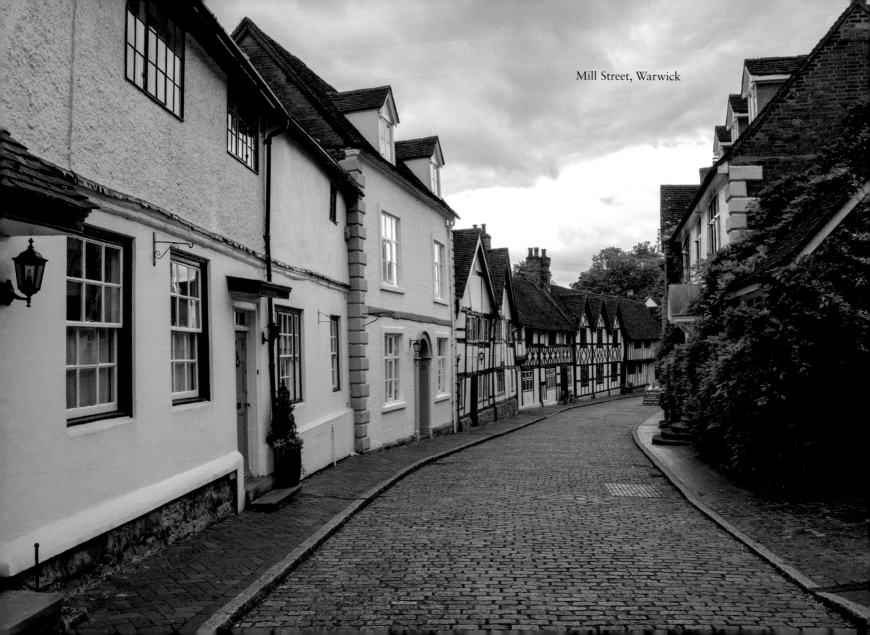

Mill Street, Warwick

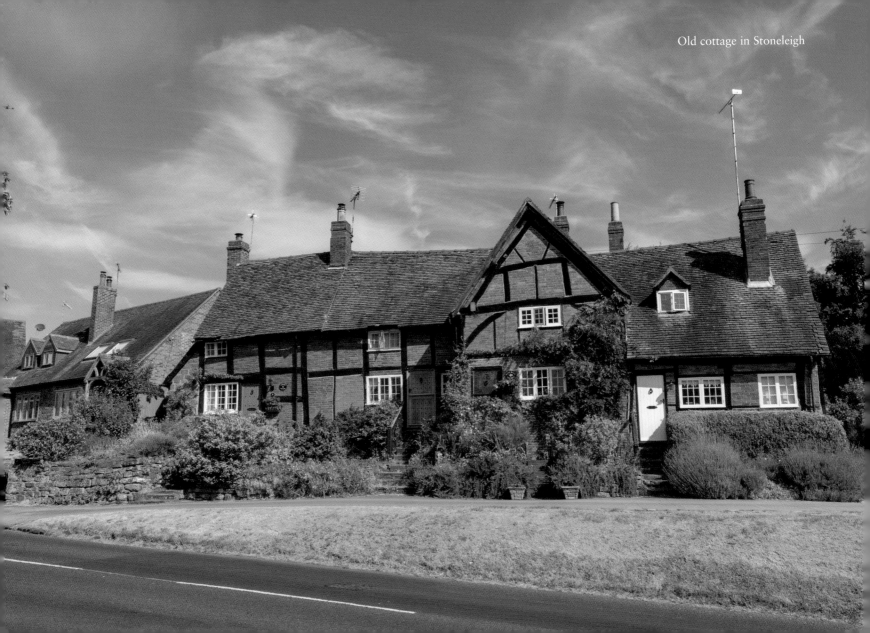

Old cottage in Stoneleigh

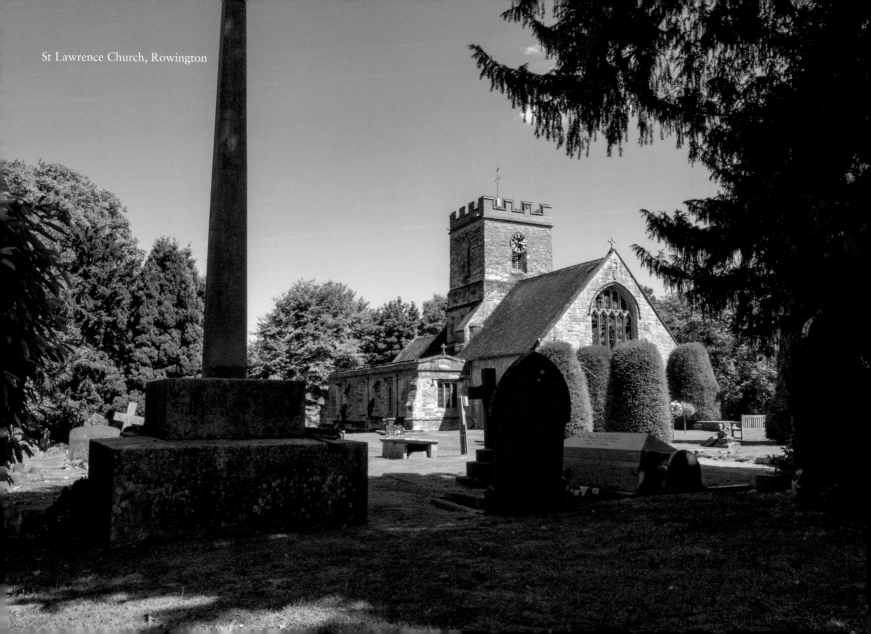

St Lawrence Church, Rowington

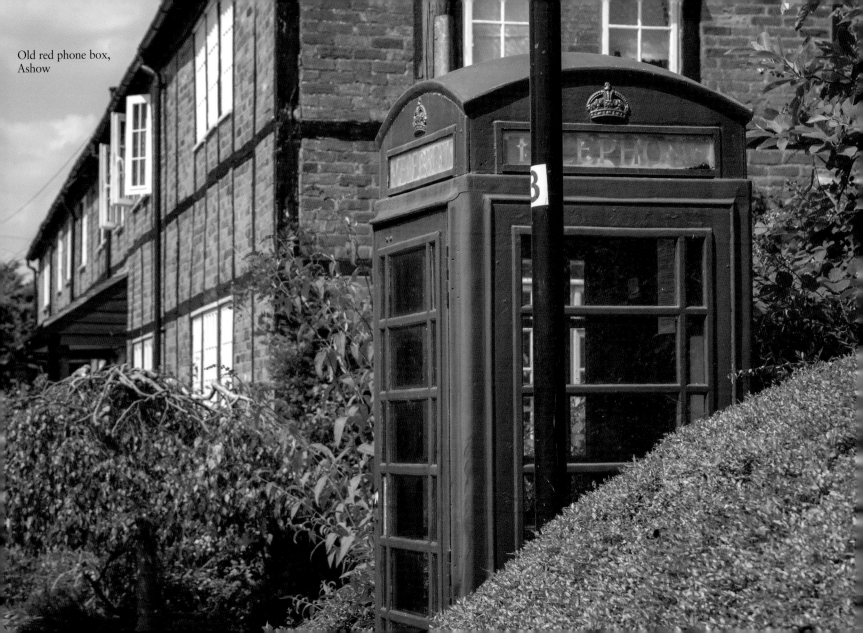

Old red phone box,
Ashow

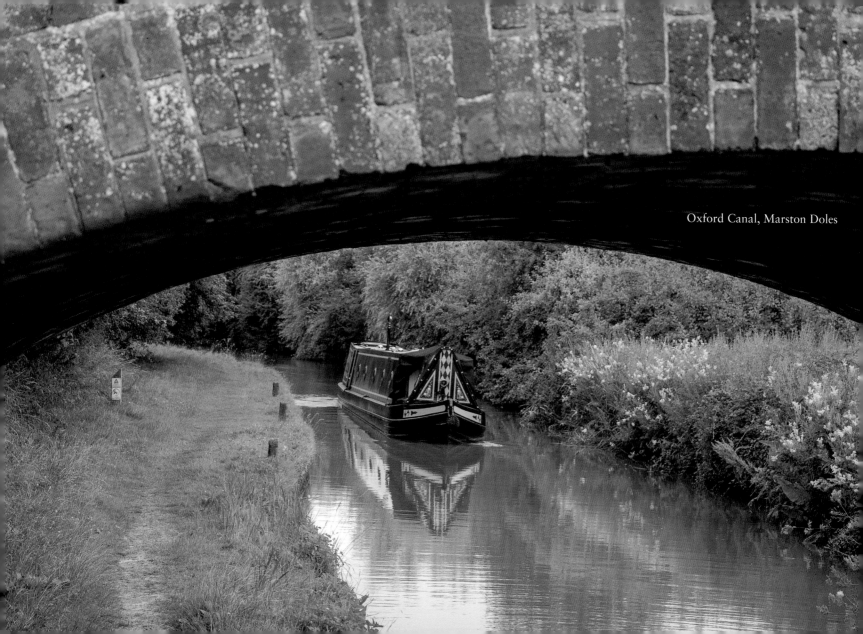

Oxford Canal, Marston Doles

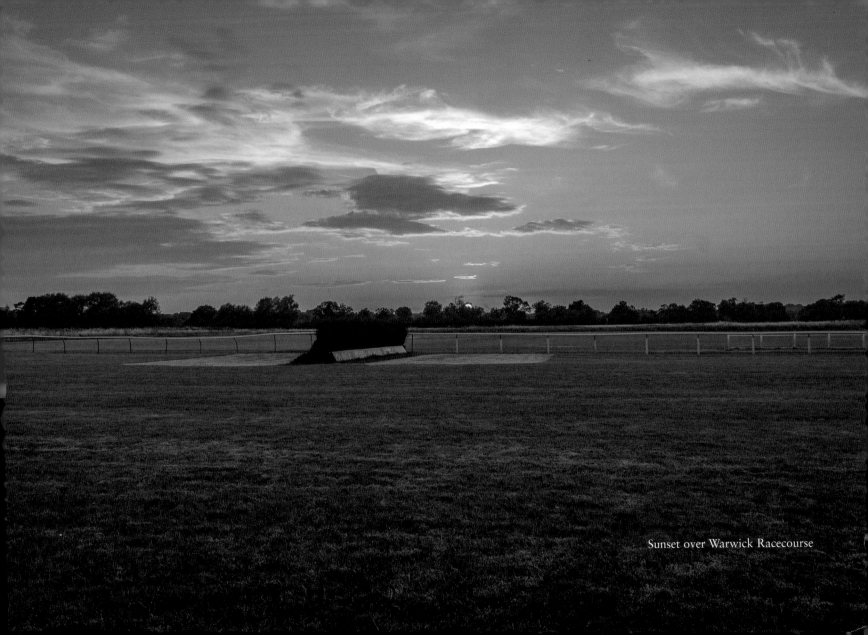

Sunset over Warwick Racecourse

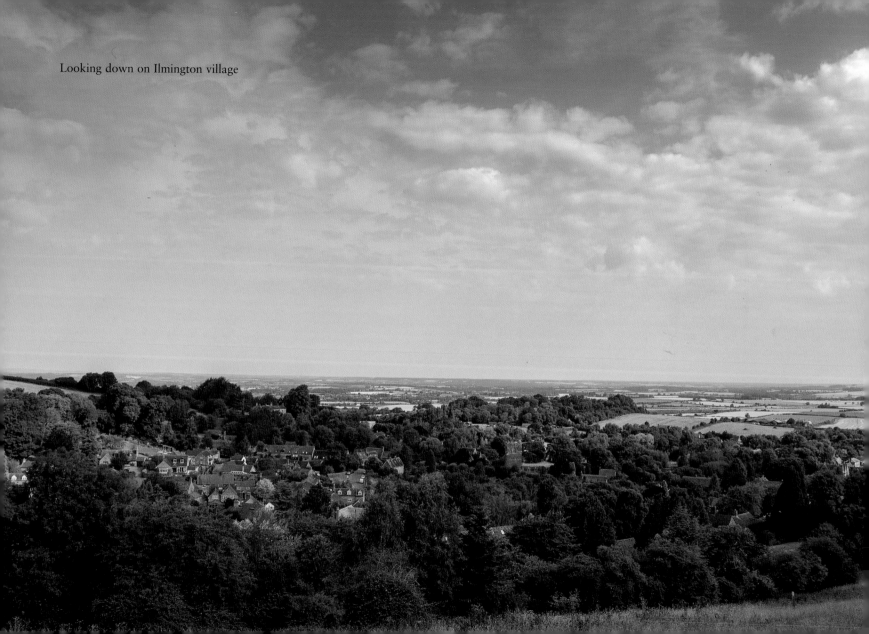

Looking down on Ilmington village